THE LITTLE BOOK OF ENVIRONMENTAL PRINCIPLES

DR PATRICK HOOK

NEW HOLLAND

Published in 2008 by New Holland Publishers (UK) Ltd
London • Cape Town • Sydney • Auckland

www.newhollandpublishers.com

Garfield House, 86–88 Edgware Road, London W2 2EA, United Kingdom
80 McKenzie Street, Cape Town 8001, South Africa
Unit 1, 66 Gibbes Street, Chatswood, NSW 2067, Australia
218 Lake Road, Northcote, Auckland, New Zealand

10 9 8 7 6 5 4 3 2 1

ISBN 978 1 84773 067 1

Publishing Director: Rosemary Wilkinson
Editors: Giselle Osborne; Aruna Vasudevan, Julia Shone
Design: Focus Publishing, Sevenoaks, Kent; Phil Kay, New Holland
Illustrator: Heather McMillan
Production: Melanie Dowland
Reproduction by Pica Digital Pte. Ltd., Singapore
Printed and bound in India by Replika Press

The paper used to produce this book is sourced from sustainable forests.

Contents

HOW TO USE THIS BOOK

The New Holland Little Books are easy-to-use comprehensive guides to important subjects. The Little Books feature over 100 entries on key principles or theories essential to understanding the subject. Written in an easily accessible manner, each Little Book explains sometimes very difficult concepts and theories, putting them in their historical context, giving background information on the experts who conceived them in the first place, analysing influences and proposing, where relevant, links to other related entries. The books also feature tables, equations, and illustrations, and end with a glossary, where relevant, and an index.

The Little Book of Environmental Principles is arranged alphabetically. Each entry includes a clear main heading, a short introductory paragraph explaining the concept or principle concisely. In some cases, the main explanation is followed by a cross reference to a linked subject. The book ends with a comprehensive index.

Other books in the series include: *The Little Book of Mathematical Principles* and *The Little Book of Medical Breakthroughs.*

The alphabetical letter under which the entry is featured on the top right or left of each page for easy access.

The entry name.

The idea in brief.

Albedo

The word 'albedo' is used to describe the amount of light that is reflected by an object.

In environmental terms, albedo is usually used to refer to the reflection of sunlight off the clouds and various atmospheric particles.

The degree to which albedo occurs has a significant influence on the amount of heat that reaches the planet. It is therefore a vital component in the system that controls the greenhouse effect.

The albedo is sometimes measured as a percentage, but for the figure to mean anything, it is important to know which part of the electromagnetic spectrum it is referring to.

Snow is one of the most reflective natural substances and typically has an albedo value of about 90 per cent. Deserts also tend to have a high overall value, whereas forests and large bodies of water, like lakes, seas and oceans, do not reflect much light. Different types of clouds, also, have differing albedo values.

There is no doubt that the Earth's albedo has been altered as a result of mankind's activities, which include cutting down forests and creating aircraft contrails. But what is not yet known is whether the overall effect is an increase or a decrease in global warming.

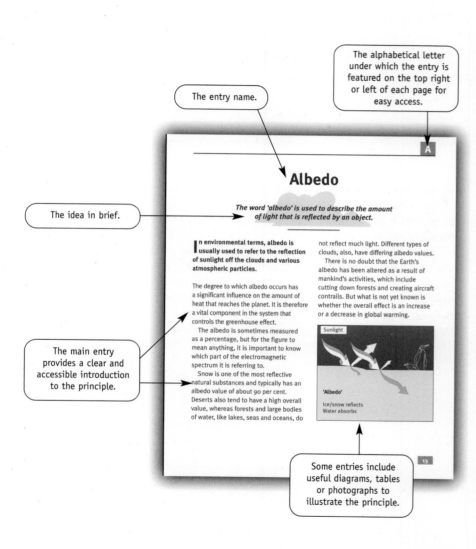

Sunlight

'Albedo'

Ice/snow reflects
Water absorbs

The main entry provides a clear and accessible introduction to the principle.

Some entries include useful diagrams, tables or photographs to illustrate the principle.

Acid Rain

*Acid rain is ordinary rain that has been
polluted with airborne chemicals such as the acidic
oxides of sulphur and nitrogen.*

**The chemicals in acid rain typically
result from the emissions produced
by industrial and domestic activity or
from volcanic eruptions.**

The expression 'acid rain' also applies
to any other form of precipitation
such as snow, sleet or hail, and can
even occur as an acid fog, although
this tends to be described as 'smog'.
These are all 'wet' forms of acid rain,
however, but there are also 'dry'
forms where the acid remains in the
atmosphere as gases and particulates.

The exact definition of acid rain can
vary depending on the predominant
local conditions. Some experts consider
it to be acidic when its pH is less than
5.6, whereas others use a figure of
5.0. Before the Industrial Revolution
(which lasted between the mid 18th and
mid 19th centuries), glacial evidence
suggests that in
some areas the
average value was
over 6.0 (the lower
the figure, the more
acidic it is).

Acid rain can cause
many environmental
problems, from
poisoning waterways
to killing plants and
animals.

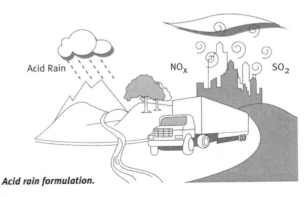

Acid rain formulation.

Agriculture

The term 'agriculture' refers to the deliberate raising of animals or plants for foodstuffs or some other kind of product.

There are several different forms of agriculture. In arable farming, for instance, crops such as grasses, grains, fruit and fibre-bearing plants are grown. Livestock farming involves rearing various kinds of animals, and can include aquaculture (fish farming), as well as cows, sheep, pigs, chickens and so on.

The third major type of agriculture is forestry, in which trees are planted and then harvested for such purposes as wood used in construction work or as pulp for the paper industry. Mixed agriculture is where a farm undertakes more than one of the above categories simultaneously.

Badly managed agriculture can have terrible consequences for the environment. In some rainforest areas, for instance, peasant farmers do not have the resources to look after their land properly. Instead, they engage in slash-and-burn techniques, in which virgin forest is repeatedly cut down and burned to make way for their crops. At the other end of the scale, intensive farming can release massive quantities of pesticides and fertilizers into the local ecosystem.

Records show that the first farmers began the planned growing of crops such as early forms of wheat, as well as hulled barley and chick peas, as far back as 9500 BC, in what is modern-day Iraq and Israel. Nowadays, farming is still one of the most common occupations around the world.

Air Pollution

The term 'air pollution' refers to various forms of atmospheric contaminant. Such materials can be chemical or biological, and may be manmade or come from natural sources.

The main gaseous pollutants of air include methane, sulphurous oxides, carbon monoxide and dioxide, various oxides of nitrogen and certain volatile organic compounds.

In addition, to the above, there are many kinds of particulate pollutants (tiny particles of solid or liquid suspended in gas), which are mostly made up of soot, smoke and dust. Large numbers of other harmful chemicals can also find their way into the atmosphere. Although the quantities involved may be small, they can have serious consequences for the environment. A good example of this is the group of chlorofluorocarbons (CFCs), compounds that contain chlorine, fluorine and carbon. These can seriously damage the ozone layer.

Certain heavy metals – including lead, iron, cadmium and copper – can also be major sources of airborne toxins. Until recently, lead tetraethyl – a major source of lead pollution – was an important constituent in gasoline fuels. However, new regulations have reduced this output significantly. Although industrial

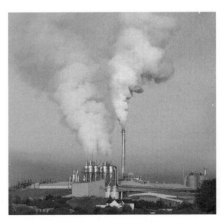

Industrial chimney stacks emitting toxic fumes into the atmosphere.

Causes of air pollution.

and domestic activities produce a great many of these materials, natural sources such as volcanoes, wildfires and marshland emissions are responsible for the vast majority.

It is also important to remember that air pollution can frequently occur indoors. In temperate climates, people spend a large proportion of their time inside their homes and offices, and they can be affected by chemicals from smoking, cooking and heating appliances, paint fumes and vapours from building materials.

Air Quality Index

The Air Quality Index is a system that is used to determine how clean the air is in a given location at a particular time.

The index ranges from 0 (no pollution at all) to over 300 (which indicates that severe amounts of toxic substances are present).

Those toxic substances measured include nitrogen, sulphur dioxides and ozone, all of which irritate the airways of the lungs, and particulate matter (fine particles) which can go deep into the lungs, causing inflammation and worsening lung disease.

There are six levels within the Air Quality Index:

1. Good: The index value is between 0 and 50, with little or no air pollution.

2. Moderate: The index value is between 51 and 100. This means that the air quality is acceptable but could still affect particularly sensitive people.

3. Unhealthy for Sensitive Groups: The index value is between 101 and 150; the air is satisfactory for healthy people, but not for those suffering from lung or heart disease.

4. Unhealthy: The index value is between 151 and 200; the air is poor and may cause health problems even for healthy people.

5. Very Unhealthy: The index value is between 201 and 300; the air can cause serious health problems.

6. Hazardous: The index value is over 300. In this case, the air is so bad that emergency warnings are likely.

Albedo

The word 'albedo' is used to describe the amount of light that is reflected by an object.

In environmental terms, albedo is usually used to refer to the reflection of sunlight off the clouds and various atmospheric particles.

The degree to which albedo occurs has a significant influence on the amount of heat that reaches the planet. It is therefore a vital component in the system that controls the greenhouse effect.

The albedo is sometimes measured as a percentage, but for the figure to mean anything, it is important to know which part of the electromagnetic spectrum it is referring to.

Snow is one of the most reflective natural substances and typically has an albedo value of about 90 per cent. Deserts also tend to have a high overall value, whereas forests and large bodies of water, like lakes, seas and oceans, do not reflect much light. Different types of clouds also have differing albedo values.

There is no doubt that the Earth's albedo has been altered as a result of humankind's activities, which include cutting down forests and creating aircraft contrails. But what is not yet known is whether the overall effect is an increase or a decrease in global warming.

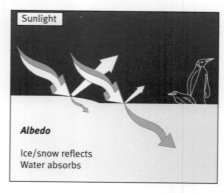

Sunlight

Albedo

Ice/snow reflects
Water absorbs

Alpine or Highland Climates

Alpine or highland climates are found at high altitudes across the world.

Alpine or highland climates in the higher latitudes tend to be very cold all year round, but those in temperate and tropical zones usually experience warm summers, with average temperatures which may be around 10°C/50°F.

During warm summers, areas with alpine climates can often be covered by vast swathes of flowering plants and may be home to many kinds of fauna, from bees and butterflies to mountain goats and eagles. In winter, however, the animals tend to move to lower areas as temperatures usually drop to around -18°C/0.4°F or lower, depending on the location.

Most alpine regions receive just 3cm/9in of precipitation, or thereabouts. Since the ground is typically steep and rocky, any rainwater washes off very quickly. As a result, alpine areas are often home to lots of small, fast-flowing streams. Any snowfall tends to accumulate during the winter without melting and then thaws in the spring.

Alpine climates occur in such areas as the Rocky Mountains in North America, the Altai in Central Asia, the Andes in South America, the Alps in Europe and the Himalayas in Tibet.

Amphibians

The animals that make up the class known as amphibians are all cold-blooded or 'ectothermic', and depend on their surroundings for their body heat.

Despite being air-breathing creatures, amphibians can absorb oxygen through their skin. The creatures included in this group are frogs, toads, newts, salamanders, caecilians and axolotls.

The ancestors of amphibians were the first vertebrates to live on land, and their life histories still reflect this evolution. Amphibians begin life as eggs that hatch into legless water-dwelling tadpoles breathing through exterior gills. At first, they feed on microscopic plants and animals, but they begin hunting aquatic invertebrates and feeding on the remains of dead animals as they grow into adults. In maturity they shed their gills and breathe through lungs.

There are around 6,000 different species of amphibians. Most spend the majority of the year on land, only returning to water to breed.

Amphibians are important to the environment, helping to control a variety of pests, including mosquitoes and slugs. They are also sensitive to the presence of environmental toxins as their skins absorb pollutants easily – and therefore they are good indicators of an ecosystem's health. In recent years, many amphibians have become extinct thanks to a fungal disease called Chytridiomycosis, which could potentially push a third of the surviving species into extinction. The causes of this pandemic are not fully understood, but could possibly be linked to human activities (including habitat loss and pollution). If the situation is not brought under control soon, there could be devastating consequences for the environment.

Anemometer

An anemometer is an instrument used by meteorologists to measure average wind speed.

Anemometers play an important role in the process of forecasting the weather and monitoring the climate.

Placed in a suitable location, the anemometer's readings are taken in knots. The recordings may then be displayed on a weather chart to show wind direction and strength. The usual symbol for wind speed is known as a 'wind barb', and the various levels are shown on the weather chart in question.

There are several different types of anemometers. Ranging in complexity, they include cup anemometers (invented in 1846 by Dr John Thomas Romney Robinson of Armagh Observatory), as well as hotwire anemometers and, the simplest of all, the windmill anemometer.

The most expensive versions are the preserve of well-funded laboratories, and operate using a principle called laser Doppler velocimetry. This measures the degree of back scatter of light from air molecules, which allows the wind speed to be determined. Another high-tech system uses ultrasonic acoustic waves to do the same job.

The term 'anemometer' is derived from the Greek word, *anemos*, meaning 'wind'. There are other anemometers that also measure wind pressure.

A cup anemometer.

Animal Kingdom

*The Animal Kingdom is the group
to which all creatures belong.*

**The technical term for the Animal
Kingdom group is 'Kingdom
Animalia' or 'Metazoa'. There are many
sub-categories, with differing
taxonomic systems using slightly
different hierarchies.**

Most animals are multi-cellular and, at
some stage in their life cycle, all are able
to move at will (the group does not
include bacteria).

Almost all animals have bodies that
are made up of a wide variety of tissue
types, such as muscles, digestive tracts,
nervous systems and so on. Aquatic and
marine sponges are an exception to this
rule, however.

The higher animals all belong to the
phylum Chordata in the subphylum
Vertebrata. Beyond this there are many
classes, families and genera, often with
subdivisions between them. Mammals,
for instance, are all in the class
Mammalia. Examples of these include
humans, dogs, cats, lions, tigers, cows,
sheep, monkeys, dolphins and whales.

Most animals undergo sexual
reproduction, although some species,
such as stick insects, provide exceptions
to this. The majority of stick insects
are female and in some species can
produce fertile eggs even without
mating. This process is known as
parthenogenesis.

Antarctic Region

The Antarctic Region is the zone enclosed by the Antarctic Circle, a line that runs around the earth at a latitude of 66° 33' south of the equator, and centred around the South Pole.

The continent of Antarctica is huge, the region is mostly comprised of seas and oceans, with a small number of tiny islands scattered across them.

Antarctica's climate is extreme, made worse by high altitude. In winter, temperatures can plunge: in 1983, the lowest figure recorded was -89.2°C/ -128.6°F, at Vostok in the Australian Antarctic Territory. The constant strong winds can reach speeds of over 322kph/200mph.

The size of the Antarctic continent changes during the year, doubling in size in mid-winter since much of the sea around it freezes into pack ice.

The Antarctic holds almost three-quarters of the world's fresh water in the form of ice; it could significantly alter sea levels if global warming continues. The consensus is that although the region's sea ice may melt more quickly, the overall temperatures of the inland areas are unlikely to change much. As sea ice floats, it does not change sea levels if it melts. Most scientific models suggest that if the area's climate rises, more snow will fall, offsetting any rises in the sea level.

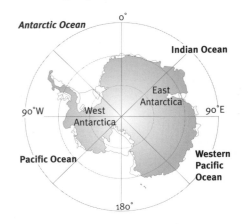

Antarctic Treaty System

The Antarctic Treaty System is a collection of agreements that came into force in 1961 to protect the region's ecosystem. It covers the area south of 60° S latitude.

Although the Antarctic region is a fierce, foreboding place with the harshest climate in the world, its ecosystem is delicately balanced.

Ever since the waters in the area were first charted in the late 19th century, humankind has been wreaking havoc with the area's marine mammal population. Many whaling and sealing ships sailed into the area and huge numbers of animals were slaughtered.

By the 1950s it was clear that drastic action was needed to prevent many species in the region from becoming extinct. It was also obvious to experts that any form of industrial activity could potentially lead to enormous environmental problems.

Unfortunately, over the years several countries claimed ownership of different parts of the region, and this led to many conflicts and counterclaims. Despite this, careful negotiations and diplomacy resulted in 12 countries agreeing to sign a number of agreements in the early 1960s. Collectively known as the 'Antarctic Treaty System', these treaties have since been significantly extended, enhancing the protection of the region's environment, flora and fauna in a number of different ways.

The treaty sets Antarctica aside as a scientific reserve, banning all military activity and nuclear testing, as well as the disposal of any radioactive waste within the Antarctic Circle. It also sets aside disputes over territorial sovereignty. The protection that the treaty has afforded the area has been an undoubted success.

Today, 46 countries – representing around 80 per cent of the world's population – have signed the treaty.

Arctic Region

*The word 'Arctic' comes from the Greek **Megas Arktos** (meaning the Great Bear) and refers to the area at the southernmost point of the Constellation Ursa Major.*

There are two main definitions as to what constitutes the Arctic Region. The first states that it is the region centred on the North Pole and enclosed by the Arctic Circle. The second defines it as the area centred on the North Pole where the warmest month has an average daily temperature of less than 10°C/50°F.

A large part of the region consists of the Arctic Ocean, while the North Pole itself is actually a long way out to sea. For most of the year the sea is frozen into a solid slab of pack ice, although much of this melts during the summer months.

Previously, it was only possible to reach the North Pole on foot at the height of summer but, in recent years, the ice has receded enough to make it possible to sail a ship there. The reasons are still unclear, but global warming is almost certainly responsible.

The extent of the Arctic's sea ice over the last few centuries is unknown, so accurate assessments of the current situation cannot be made. Average temperatures have risen at about twice the rate of those of the rest of the world over the last two decades, however. This statement must be viewed in context though, as the ice also melted during the Medieval Warm Period (c. 800–1300 AD).

Although global sea levels are not affected by changes in the amount of sea ice, the Arctic's glaciers hold more than 3 million km^3/0.7 million mi^3 of ice. If these melted it would have a massive impact on the world's environment, with many low-lying areas becoming permanently inundated.

Asbestos

The word 'asbestos' comes from the Greek term for 'inextinguishable' and relates to a collection of naturally occurring fibrous silicate minerals.

Asbestos fibres, which may measure less than a micron in diameter, are soft and easily worked into fabrics. This, combined with their ability to withstand heat, made materials containing asbestos popular with the Greeks and Romans.

Asbestos became popular in the United Kingdom during the industrialization of the 19th century, due to its strength and fire-resistant properties, and by the 1950s it was widely used in property building and such industries as shipbuilding and car manufacturing.

Over the last 30 years, however, its dangers have become increasingly apparent. Inhaling the fibres can cause horrific diseases, including asbestosis and cancers such as mesothelioma. Consequently, the use of asbestos has become heavily regulated across most of the developed world.

Some forms of asbestos are much more dangerous than others. Those that are blended with cement, for instance, are only hazardous if they are broken up and the dust is released into the air. White asbestos, which is obtained from some kinds of serpentine rocks, is banned in many countries. Blue asbestos, which is extracted from the mineral riebeckite,

is considered to be even more dangerous.

There are many other kinds of asbestos, as well as related substances, which are called 'asbestiform' minerals.

Atmosphere

The atmosphere is a layer of gases that envelops the Earth and primarily comprises nitrogen (78 per cent) and oxygen (21 per cent).

At sea level there is an average pressure of about 14.7 lbf (literally, pounds of force) and, for scientific purposes, there is a unit called the standard atmosphere, which has a value of 101.325 kPa (kilopascals, a unit for measuring atmospheric pressure). This equates to 760mm Hg/29.92in Hg (Hg refers to mercury used to measure the partial pressure of a gas).

As altitude increases the pressure quickly falls off, and although the atmosphere is about 560km/350mi thick, there is only enough oxygen for humans to survive for about the first 6.4km/4mi closest to the Earth's surface.

The atmosphere's provision of breathable air is not the only factor making it essential for life as it performs other vital functions, too. For a start, it shields the Earth's surface from ultraviolet radiation, and acts as an insulator from the freezing vacuum of outer space. It also allows water to evaporate and then accumulate before returning to the surface as precipitation, and acts to render many toxic gases harmless.

Although planet Earth has been around for some 4.5 billion years, the atmosphere has only existed in a form able to support life for about 570 million years.

High Pressure Centres

Also known as anticyclones, high pressure centres are the zones of highest pressure in a given area. On weather maps they are indicated by a blue 'H'.

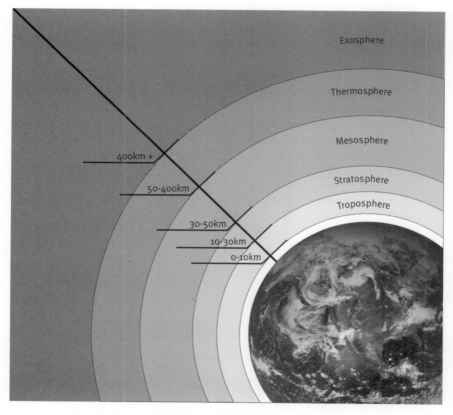

The above illustration shows the various layers of the Earth's atmosphere.

Aurora Borealis

This is a spectacular optical effect of the reaction between solar radiation and high-altitude atmospheric particles.

Also known as the Northern Lights, the Aurora Borealis occurs in the night skies near the North Pole between September and October and again in March and April. A similar effect seen near the South Pole is called the Southern Lights, or Aurora Australis.

The Aurora Borealis is named after Aurora, the Roman goddess of the dawn, and Boreas, from the Greek god of the north wind. It is caused by the collision of ions (charged particles) with atoms of gas in the Earth's upper atmosphere. This often happens when sunspot

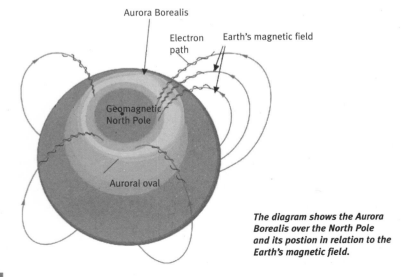

The diagram shows the Aurora Borealis over the North Pole and its postion in relation to the Earth's magnetic field.

A spectacular example of the Aurora Borealis, as seen over Alaska, United States.

activity is high. The atoms gain in energy, emitting this as light and producing intense arrays of colour that move around in a blaze of red, green, blue and violet. These lights often appear as curtains, which are made from parallel rays lined up with magnetic field lines. This is cited as evidence for the theory that aurorae are controlled by the Earth's magnetism.

The energy involved in these spectacular displays is immense. Around a million megawatts are consumed by the more vivid auroras. This activity has the potential to create significant electromagnetic interference, capable of disabling or even destroying such vital electrical devices as power line distribution systems or telecommunications equipment. Now, though, using research into the physics of sunspots and auroras, it is possible to predict their occurrences with greater accuracy than previously.

Beaufort Scale

The Beaufort Windforce Scale, invented by Sir Francis Beaufort in 1805, helps estimate wind speeds based on the various effects that are observed.

The scale has two different lists of visual indicators, one for land and one for sea. Each has 13 categories, rising from 0 to 12.

B'ft No.	Speed MPH	Speed Knots	Description	Observed Effects on Land
0	0–1	0–1	CALM	Calm; smoke rises vertically.
1	1–3	1–3	LIGHT AIR	Wind direction indicated by smoke drift, but not by wind vanes.
2	4–7	4–6	LIGHT BREEZE	Wind felt on face; leaves rustle; vanes moved by wind.
3	8–12	7–10	GENTLE BREEZE	Leaves and small twigs move constantly; light flags extended.
4	13–18	11–16	MODERATE BREEZE	Dust and loose paper raised; small branches are moved.
5	19–24	17–21	FRESH BREEZE	Small trees in leaf begin to sway.
6	25–31	22–27	STRONG BREEZE	Large tree branches in motion; whistling heard in telephone cables.
7	32–38	28–33	NEAR GALE	Whole trees begin to move; inconvenience felt when walking.
8	39–46	34–40	GALE	Twigs and small branches broken off trees.
9	47–54	41–47	SEVERE GALE	Slight structural damage; large branches broken off trees.
10	55–63	48–55	STORM	Seldom experienced on land; trees uprooted; significant structural damage.
11	64–72	56–63	VIOLENT STORM	Widespread damage.
12	73–83	64–71	HURRICANE	Catastrophic damage experienced.

THE BEAUFORT SCALE – EFFECTS OF THE WIND ON LAND

Beaufort Number 0, for instance, is applied where there is no wind at all – smoke rises vertically, and the surface of the sea is like a mirror. At the other end of the scale, Beaufort Number 12 is used for hurricanes with wind speeds of over 117kph/73mph. On land this is marked by catastrophic damage. At sea, visibility is very poor, the air is completely filled with foam and spray, while the sea itself is white with driving spray.

THE BEAUFORT SCALE – EFFECTS OF THE WIND ON THE SEA				
B'ft No.	**Speed MPH**	**Speed Knots**	**Description at Sea**	**Observed Effects**
0	0–1	0–1	CALM	Sea like a mirror.
1	1–3	1–3	LIGHT AIR	Scale-like ripples, but without foam crests.
2	4–7	4–6	LIGHT BREEZE	Small wavelets that do not break.
3	8–12	7–10	GENTLE BREEZE	Large wavelets with crests that begin to break. Some scattered white horses.
4	13–18	11–16	MODERATE BREEZE	Small waves, with frequent white horses.
5	19–24	17–21	FRESH BREEZE	Moderate waves – many white horses and some spray.
6	25–31	22–27	STRONG BREEZE	Large waves with white foam and crests with moderate spray.
7	32–38	28–33	NEAR GALE	Sea heaps up and white foam is blown from crests in the direction of the wind.
8	39–46	34–40	GALE	Moderately high waves of greater length; crests begin to break into spindrift. Foam is blown in streaks in the direction of the wind.
9	47–54	41–47	SEVERE GALE	High waves. Dense streaks of foam blown along by the wind. Heavy spray.
10	55–63	48–55	STORM	Very high waves with over-hanging crests. The sea takes on a white appearance due to the amount of foam. Heavy rolling and visibility affected.
11	64–72	56–63	VIOLENT STORM	Exceptionally high waves and sea covered with white patches of foam. Wave crests blown into froth. Visibility further affected.
12	73–83	64–71	HURRICANE	Air completely filled with foam and spray. Sea white with driving spray; visibility very poor.

Biodegrade

The term 'biodegrade' is used to describe the way that certain substances break down into their component parts over time.

This process may take place as the result of chemical activity such as oxidative or other reduction reactions, or it may involve their physical decomposition by various organisms such as bacteria, small invertebrates or fungi.

The biodegradability of an item is an important measure of how its disposal will affect the environment. To get a realistic picture, it is important to ensure that its original packaging is included in any assessment.

Most natural products break down relatively quickly. However, those containing large amounts of lignin or cellulose fibres may persist for considerable amounts of time. This should not be a cause for concern, as they form a natural part of the ecosystem and will eventually revert to their component form.

Although many commonly used materials, such as plastics, do not biodegrade within practical timeframes, new environmentally friendly types have recently been developed that will readily decompose under certain influences.

These include substances which quickly break down in industrial composting facilities, as well as others that degrade when exposed to daylight, naturally occurring micro-organisms or by direct contact with air or water.

Examples of products that can be made in this way range from carrier bags to fast-food packaging and various types of drinks containers.

Biodiversity

There are many different definitions of 'biodiversity', but broadly the term describes the range of different life forms that can be found in a given location or region.

The natural biodiversity of a particular ecosystem can vary dramatically.

In the frozen deserts of inner Antarctica, for instance, the number of different organisms that can survive is extremely limited, with only a few soil-dwelling nematode worms and simple algae being found.

At the other end of the scale, tropical rainforests can literally teem with life. From the ground below to the air above, there are so many plants and animals that scientists have barely begun to scratch the surface in identifying and understanding them all.

When an ecosystem is subjected to some form of environmental pressure, its biodiversity usually suffers, and the extent to which this happens over time can be used as a measure of the likely long-term effects.

There are various subdivisions such as 'genetic diversity', which expresses the variations in the gene pool of a given species or population, and 'ecosystem diversity', which covers the number of different types of ecosystems in a region.

Biogas

Biogas is a combustible material that is produced as a by-product of the decomposition of organic matter.

Also referred to as marsh gas, landfill gas and swamp gas, biogas may be derived from various sources including agricultural wastes such as manure, human sewage treatment facilities, or from industrial activities.

There are two main methods of extracting biogas from the above substances. One of these uses large vessels – known as digesters – to make individual batches, whereas the other method is based on a continuous flow process. After the gas is removed, the remaining material can be used as a nutrient-rich fertilizer.

Biogas is primarily composed of methane and carbon dioxide and it

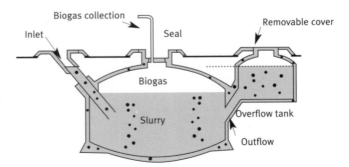

The above diagram shows the process of extracting biogas from various sources using a dome-shaped digester. These are commonly used throughout China.

The image above shows a biogas treatment facility in Germany. Matter is fermented in a storage facility (above middle) and as a result of this process gases, mainly methane and carbon dioxide, are produced and collected.

therefore burns readily. It can be used to power various devices and examples include automobile engines, heating systems or electricity generators.

Most modern landfill sites are designed to exploit the large amounts of biogas that are produced as the waste they contain decomposes. One of the side benefits is that it burns relatively cleanly, producing fewer pollutants than most equivalent fuels.

Since most of the carbon released is derived from recent plant activity, the overall negative impact of this process on the environment is far less damaging than that produced by burning fossil fuels. As methane is also one of the most damaging greenhouse gases, it makes good environmental sense to use biogas wherever it is economically practical to do so.

Biomass

The term 'biomass' refers to various kinds of organic materials that are used as sustainable fuels or as ingredients in commercial products.

Biomass substances are all carbon-rich, having absorbed significant quantities of carbon dioxide from the atmosphere while they were alive. These do not include those that have been dead for any significant length of time, such as oil or coal. This is because their use releases carbon dioxide, which is not part of the historic carbon cycle.

The use of biomass materials is often referred to as being carbon neutral, but this is only true if they are replaced by equivalent carbon-bearing animals or plants after harvesting and use. The five main types of biomass are: wood, fuel crops and farming waste, leftover food, landfill gas and alcohol fuels.

Wood is primarily obtained from commercial forestry operations, especially those based on coniferous plantations. Some deciduous species are also harvested – poplar and willow are amongst the fastest-growing examples. Fuel crops include such plants as hemp, maize, sugarcane and elephant grass.

Biomass can also be used in a variety of other applications. Houses, for instance, can be built out of straw bales and cellulose fibres used to make paper. Since biomass materials are so environmentally friendly, a great deal of research is being conducted into developing new applications, as well as finding better and more efficient ways of using them.

Biome

The term 'biome' refers to large ecosystems and encapsulates all the fauna and flora of a given location or region, in addition to the complex environmental factors influencing them.

There are many different kinds of biomes, from terrestrial ones such as deserts, rainforests, grasslands and tundra, to those that are aquatic, such as lakes and oceans.

One of the major determinants of a particular biome's characteristics is its local climate. Areas with high average temperatures and significant amounts of rainfall, for instance, tend to have the greatest levels of biodiversity.

Others may have combinations of climates and geological conditions that favour particular kinds of vegetation and this, in turn, attracts certain animals. For example, regions in medium to high latitudes with thin soil and low average temperatures tend to be covered by coniferous forests where low scrub grows under tall pine trees. This may support herbivores such as deer and rabbits, on which such predators as eagles and wolves then feed.

Many biomes have names that are specific to particular regions: examples include the Asian steppes, the pampas of South America and the South African veldt.

Humankind's activities can have severe implications for biomes and it is important that these are preserved. The oceans, for example, contain millions of plankton responsible for much of the world's photosynthetic activity. This provides vital, life-sustaining oxygen.

Bioremediation

The term 'bioremediation' describes various processes whereby natural systems are used to remove pollutants from the environment.

Bioremediation includes the use of plants to absorb heavy metal contaminants or salt from agricultural land, as well as the exploitation of microbes to break down accidental spills of such hydrocarbons as petrol, oil and diesel.

The efficiency of many of these systems has been improved significantly through

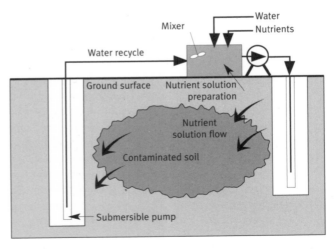

Bioremediation at work: This is the process of using naturally occurring or cultivated organisms to break down organic contaminants such as petrol, oil and diesel that are present in soil and/or water.

the use of genetic engineering. Some bacteria, for example, have been modified to help decompose certain radioactive waste materials.

The speed at which the remediation occurs can be increased by adding nutrients to the soil, as well as by ensuring that the temperature, amount of moisture, the availability of oxygen as well as the soil acidity, remain within favourable limits. Where plants are used for this purpose, they are often harvested and then incinerated to concentrate the relevant components, making it easier to render them harmless to the environment.

Examples of the many toxic materials that are removed in this manner include cadmium, mercury and lead, all of which can cause severe ecosystem problems, such as reducing breeding success in many organisms or even contributing to localized extinctions.

Bioremediation is often the most cost-effective way to clean up large-scale or hard-to-access sites, especially those where groundwater contamination is a problem. For most people, composting is probably the most familiar form of bioremediation, an everyday process in many gardens.

Biosphere

The expression 'biosphere' refers to the sum of all the places on Earth in which life exists. It is sometimes also called the 'ecosphere'.

The biosphere includes the land, freshwater, sea and air, as well as soil or rocks within which organisms live. The biosphere also covers all the ways in which they interact, along with all the underlying physical factors such as climate, geology, environmental pollutants and so on.

The exact boundaries at which life does and does not occur are very difficult to determine. Working towards the Earth's core, life begins at some point high in the atmosphere, where wind-blown pollen and fungal spores may be found.

Moving downwards, the level of diversity increases through the zone where birds and insects fly. At ground level a vast range of fauna and flora may be found, although this depends on the actual location.

Rainforests, for example, have the greatest amount of diversity, and the Antarctic deserts the least. The upper parts of the world's seas and oceans teem with life, and this diminishes with depth. Although little is known about the microbes living in the rocks deep beneath us, their combined mass could be greater than that of all the plants and animals on the surface.

Birds

Birds can be characterized as two-legged, egg-laying, warm-blooded animals with feathers, a beak (with no teeth) and a skeleton.

The first birds evolved from dinosaurs over 150 million years ago; the earliest example was a creature known as Archaeopteryx.

Analysis using the latest scientific techniques has shown that the most famous dinosaur of all – *Tyrannosaurus rex* – had protein structures that were close to those found today in chickens and ostriches.

All birds reproduce by laying eggs and have backbones as well as scaly feet. They are warm-blooded, but are distinguished from other animals by the fact that they have feathers. These lightweight structures are made from a strong protein called keratin and are typically used for flight, as well as to provide thermal insulation.

Not all birds can fly. Some evolve to fit into particular niches where flight is not necessary. The better-known examples of such birds are penguins, ostriches, rheas and emus.

Birds are classified in the Kingdom Animalia, phylum Chordata, subphylum Vertebrata and the class Aves. Within this, there are about 30 orders and about 180 families, with around 2,000 genera and about 10,000 different species. The exact figure keeps changing, however, as various subspecies are reclassified.

Carbon Cycle

During the carbon cycle, carbon is released into the atmosphere, trapped by plants or chemical processes and later released into the air again.

The carbon cycle is described as having four major, interconnected components or 'reservoirs' of carbon. These include the atmosphere, the world's biomass, the oceans and accumulated sediments (including oil and coal).

Carbon is a highly abundant element within the universe and on Earth – it is at the root of all known life. Carbon moves through the cycle as the result of a large number of natural processes, including animal and plant growth, death and decomposition.

The greatest carbon-bearing component in the atmosphere is the greenhouse gas carbon dioxide (CO_2). Although its overall percentage is very low – at around 0.04 per cent – it nevertheless makes a significant contribution to global warming.

Several other atmospheric gases also contain carbon: examples of these include methane as well as the chlorofluorocarbons. Atmospheric carbon dioxide is also absorbed from the air, as a function of plant photosynthesis, and this also releases oxygen back into the air.

Many of humankind's activities generate and release large amounts of carbon into the atmosphere, particularly through the burning of fossil fuels and the manufacture of industrial products. Volcanic activity is also a major source, with enormous volumes of carbon dioxide released every time there is an eruption.

It has been calculated that the amount of carbon dioxide in the atmosphere has increased by nearly a third since the beginning of the Industrial Revolution about 250 years ago.

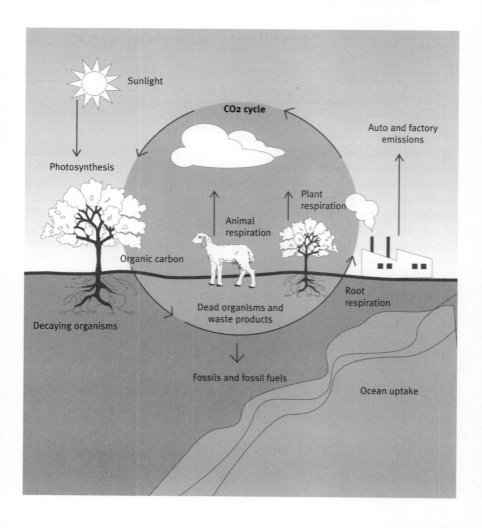

Sunlight

CO2 cycle

Auto and factory emissions

Photosynthesis

Plant respiration

Animal respiration

Organic carbon

Root respiration

Decaying organisms

Dead organisms and waste products

Fossils and fossil fuels

Ocean uptake

Carbon Monoxide & Carbon Dioxide

*The two main oxides of carbon are
carbon monoxide and carbon dioxide.*

Although these gases are quite similar (colourless, odourless and tasteless) carbon monoxide and carbon dioxide have many different properties from an environmental perspective.

Carbon monoxide, which is composed of a single carbon atom bonded to a single oxygen atom, is a toxic and inflammable gas. It can be released naturally into the atmosphere from such events as bushfires, volcanoes and other geological activity.

Humankind's activities are also responsible for large quantities of the gas reaching the environment. Chief among these are the gases produced by burning fossil fuels such as petrol, diesel, paraffin and coal. Although carbon monoxide is a recognized pollutant, it does not last long in the atmosphere before being converted into carbon dioxide.

This is composed of a single carbon atom bonded to two oxygen atoms and is a non-toxic, non-flammable gas. It is, however, one of the primary greenhouse gases, mostly due to its ability to absorb heat from the Sun's rays. This makes it a significant contributor to global warming, despite the fact that it only occurs in the atmosphere at a concentration of about 385 parts per million.

The above picture shows an internationally recognised symbol alerting people to the dangers of carbon monoxide.

Carcinogens

Carcinogens are materials or other agents that can cause or worsen any form of cancer.

As well as X-rays and ultraviolet radiation from the Sun, carcinogens include a large number of everyday substances. Harmful chemicals such as formaldehyde, vinyl chloride and benzene are good examples of these.

There are many different kinds of cancers and they can occur in almost any part of the body, affecting many different species. They are usually characterized by tumours or other structures that grow out of control, and may be initiated by some form of damage to the DNA within particular cells.

This damage may result from exposure to a wide range of harmful chemicals such as those listed above. Alternatively, carcinogens may be inhaled, and particularly hazardous in this respect are tobacco smoke, certain pesticides and asbestos.

The Sun's ultraviolet rays are carcinogenic, but eating food that contains carcinogenic agents is a very common way of coming into contact with them. Scientific studies seem to suggest that a variety of over-cooked fats, carbohydrates and proteins should be avoided, where possible, as should the charring on barbecued meat.

Infection with certain viruses (such as hepatitis B and the human papilloma viruses) have been known to cause cancers, although research in this area is still ongoing.

Carnivore

*A carnivore is an organism that feeds on
the body tissue of other animals.*

There are various definitions that
may or may not include species
that feed on creatures like insects
(insectivores) or the bodies of dead
animals (scavengers).

Not all carnivores are animals. Many
plants deliberately set out to entrap
animals and then digest them: these
include Venus fly traps, sundews,
butterworts and pitcher plants. There are
even fungi that feed on soil microbes
and other microscopic creatures.

In cases in which an animal eats
members of its own species, this is
referred to as cannibalism. The most
common example of this is when an
adult eats its young. Many predatory
fish, for instance, make no distinction
between the young (fry) of their own and
that of other species.

Some plant-eating animals
resort to cannibalism under certain
circumstances, particularly if their
numbers increase beyond a certain
point. This is a natural form of control
that helps to prevent problems
associated with high population
densities, such as disease, habitat
destruction and increases in predators.

There is an order within the animal
kingdom called the 'Carnivora'. These
include dogs, cats, bears, wolves,
civets and foxes. Although they are
primarily meat-eaters, some only eat
vegetation: the Giant Panda, for
instance, eats just bamboo leaves.

Carnivores are extremely vital to the
environment, providing natural control
for herbivores and omnivores which
would otherwise reproduce beyond the
capacity of their own local ecosystems.

Cephalopods

Cephalopods are marine invertebrates which belong to the same phylum as slugs and snails – that is, the molluscs.

Many millions of years ago cephalopods were one of the predominant life forms on Earth, and their first ancestors probably developed in the late Cambrian period.

The rise of large predators cut the reign of the cephalopods short. Although there have been around 11,000 different species since this time, there are now only about 1,200 living forms left.

In modern times cephalopods are represented by four groups: the nautilus, squid, cuttlefish and octopus. Apart from the six species of nautilus, all have lost their shells over time.

Cephalopods are thought to be the most intelligent of all the invertebrates, having large brains and excellent vision. Some have complex social structures including colour-changing skin that can convey complicated messages, although this is just one of several communication mechanisms that they have evolved.

All the members of this class are hunters, found in all the world's seas. They vary in size from small octopi, which are a few centimetres long, to the Colossal Squid (*Mesonychoteuthis hamiltoni*) which can reach lengths of over 14m/45ft.

Cetaceans

The group of creatures covered by the order Cetacea includes whales, porpoises and dolphins.

Although these highly intelligent animals live in water – usually the sea – they are not fish, but, in fact, air-breathing mammals.

Until relatively recently, cetaceans were simply perceived as a commodity to be harvested and, as a consequence, were ruthlessly hunted for their meat and oil content. This resulted in the populations of certain species plummeting. If international pressure had not been applied to the countries responsible for this depletion in stocks, many of these creatures would, in all probability, be extinct by now.

Fortunately, these majestic creatures are now so popular that people are willing to pay large sums of money to view them first-hand in their natural habitats. This has spawned a new industry, whale-watching ecotourism, which has provided former whalers not just with a new source of income, but also a vested interest in keeping whales alive.

Cetaceans fall into two basic lifestyle categories: those that actively hunt fish and those that filter feed on plankton. This latter category includes the largest animal species ever to have lived, the Blue Whale(*Balaenoptera musculus*)which can reach 33m/110ft in length and a weight of 180MT/200T.

The Blue Whale, also known as **Balaenoptera musculus**

Chemical Accident

Chemical accidents often feature the unintentional release of poisonous and hazardous materials, involving fires or explosions.

Accidents sometimes occur during the manufacture, storage, use or transportation of hazardous/dangerous materials. In fact, such mishaps have occurred since the beginning of the Bronze Age, when humankind began working with metal, smelting copper and tin and mixing these to cast bronze.

In prehistoric times, the operations were on a minor scale and the environmental consequences were generally rather limited. As time went on, however, the scale of manufacturing grew and the Industrial Revolution (c. 1750–1850) ushered in a new era of environmental damage. The factories that sprang up in large towns and cities used coal to heat water to produce steam to power their machines. Burning coal produces black smoke which often covered the streets like a thick, dirty blanket and became a major cause of urban air pollution.

At the time, all manner of hazardous chemicals were used without regard for the safety of the workers involved, or the surrounding countryside. Such materials as arsenic were common in the workplace, as were accidents resulting in spillages of toxic materials. As a result, the wildlife in local rivers in industrialized places was soon killed off.

In the 20th century, industry in the developed world has become heavily regulated and accidents are much rarer. Sadly, this is not the case in the emerging economies, and in some places deaths, injuries and widespread environmental poisoning still occur. One of the worst accidents occurred in 1984 at the Union Carbide pesticide plant in Bhopal, India, when a release of methyl isocyanate gas killed over 2,000 people. Since then, many more people have been diagnosed with diseases allegedly related to the accident, including cancer.

Chlorofluorocarbon

Chlorofluorocarbons, which are also known as CFCs, are one of the world's better-known atmospheric pollutants.

CFCs first came to world prominence in the 1970s, when they were found to be responsible for creating holes in the ozone layer over the polar regions.

In the past 35 years or so, CFCs have also been recognized as one of the most harmful greenhouse gases; they are thousands of times more destructive than carbon dioxide. CFCs are compounds containing chlorine, fluorine and carbon. Chemically, they are categorized as haloalkanes and are very stable. This makes them one of the most persistent pollutants and also means that it can take as long as a century for them to break down in the atmosphere.

This is unfortunate because they were used in a wide variety of commercial products until recently. These include refrigerators, fire extinguishers, dry cleaning solvents and aerosol propellants.

The use of CFCs in commercial products has been more or less banned by a series of regulations, with the first implemented in Oregon, USA, in 1975. Since then, far more wide-reaching laws have been passed. The most influential has been the Montreal Protocol on Substances that Deplete the Ozone Layer, which came into force on 1 January 1989. This has since been revised many times but its agenda remains to phase out the production and use of CFCs until these harmful toxins are eliminated altogether.

Kofi Annan, the seventh Secretary-General of the United Nations (UN), reportedly described the Montreal Protocol as *'perhaps the single most successful international agreement to date...'*.

Chlorophyll

Chlorophyll is the pigment that makes plants green; its function is to make photosynthesis possible.

Photosynthesis is a process in which sunlight is converted into energy from carbon dioxide and water, and oxygen is created as a waste product.

In photosynthesis, energy is produced in the form of glucose sugar, which is a carbohydrate either used directly to power metabolic processes or which is converted into starch and stored for later use.

There are several different kinds of chlorophyll, all of which have a feature called a porphyrin ring at the centre of their chemical structures, to which a long hydrocarbon chain is attached.

This format is similar in many ways to the functional part of the haemoglobin molecule found in human blood.

The green pigment seen in the leaves of plants is actually a mixture of two different types – chlorophylls *a* and *b*. Each of these absorbs different wavelengths of the light produced by the Sun. Type *a* is also present in green algae and certain cyanobacteria, with types *c*, *d* and *e* found in algae and protistan microbes.

The name 'chlorophyll' comes from the ancient Greek words '*chloros*', which means 'green', and '*phyllon*', which means 'leaf'.

Circadian Rhythm

The expression 'circadian rhythm' describes the daily cycle of many living things; it is usually about 24 hours long.

The circadian rhythm is the result of organisms evolving to synchronize their activities with the changes in light levels caused by the Earth's rotation.

The circadian rhythm is an important component in the regulation of such primary functions as sleeping and eating; it is relatively independent of external factors such as daylight length. The cycle is usually synchronized by environmental cues, for example, sunrise or sunset, although some animals that live underground do not need this stimulus.

In humans, the circadian clock is controlled by a pair of tiny structures called the *suprachiasmatic nucleus*. These contain about 20,000 neurons and are located in a region in the brain called the hypothalamus. They control the sleep–wake cycle, as well as the temperature regulation and endocrine systems. If the circadian rhythm is disturbed, as a result of jet-lag, for example, this can cause a variety of sleep disorders.

Treatment can include taking exercise, implementing a regular sleep-regime and avoiding stimulants such as tobacco, alcohol and drugs, as well as such caffeine-rich foodstuffs as coffee and chocolate.

Many plants use the circadian rhythm to regulate important functions such as moisture levels, the timing of petal opening, scent release and leaf movements.

CITES

CITES is an acronym for the Washington Convention on International Trade in Endangered Species of Wild Fauna and Flora.

A large number of the world's plants and animals are in danger of becoming extinct as a result of their being bought and sold by dealers and collectors. CITES helps to regulate this.

In the 1960s a group of concerned parties began lobbying for such trade to be controlled, and after several years of discussion, an agreement came into force on 1 July 1975. This is generally referred to as CITES.

More than 160 countries have signed the agreement, which is voluntary. It currently covers over 33,000 different species, and some 25,000 of these are endangered plants.

As well as controlling the export and trade in live animals and plants, CITES also covers their constituent parts, including bones, skins, seeds, roots, and any products derived from them.

Examples of protected animals covered by the convention include the Giant Panda, apes, lemurs, cheetahs, tigers, elephants, rhinos, certain monkeys, birds of prey, parrots, sea turtles, crocodiles, lizards and even creatures such as mussels, frogs and leeches. Regulated plants include certain orchids, cycads and cacti.

Travellers can be fined for importing souvenirs made from banned substances, such as tortoiseshell, ivory and reptile-skin handbags, without a valid permit.

Although it has not completely stopped trafficking in these species, CITES has nevertheless done a great deal to protect vital endangered flora and fauna from extinction.

Climate

The word 'climate' – which comes from the Greek klima *– is a way of describing the long-term weather pattern of a region.*

The world's range of climates is incredibly diverse. There are different ways to classify this, with most climates being labelled according to the predominant weather conditions experienced there.

The main global climate zones are the tropical, subtropical, temperate, sub-Arctic and Arctic. There are further subdivisions based on local environments – and in particular temperature levels and how much precipitation (rain and snow) is received. Examples of these include desert, oceanic, Mediterranean and alpine climates.

The tropical zone, for instance, is characterized by consistently high temperatures throughout the year combined with heavy rainfall. Tropical rainforests, including for example those in the Amazon Basin, Central Africa or Northern Australia, cover about 40 per cent of the Earth's surface and are a haven for many plants and animals.

Temperate climates are those where there are no extremes of temperature or precipitation, and include, for example, the central parts of the United States and Europe. In between the two there is the sub-tropical zone, where the temperature does not fall below freezing point, and rainfall is spread throughout the year. Between the temperate and polar regions lie the sub-Arctic and sub-Antarctic zones where temperatures are above 10°C/50°F for at least one, and no more than three, months of the year.

The Arctic and Antarctic regions, which are permanently covered with snow and ice, are the coldest places on Earth.

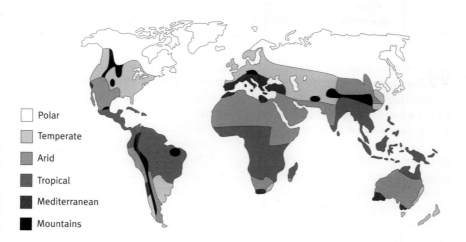

☐	Polar
▨	Temperate
▨	Arid
▨	Tropical
▨	Mediterranean
■	Mountains

Climate zones of the world.

See: *Alpine or Highland Climates*, page 14; *Arctic Region*, page 20; *Deserts*, page 66; *Environment*, page 77; *Global Warming*, pages 96–97; *Mediterranean (Chaparral) Climate*, page 124; *Oceans*, page 138; *Tropical Rainforests*, page 189

Clouds

Clouds are comprised of a collection of condensed droplets that are visible in the skies above the Earth.

When water evaporates, it usually does so as the result of heating by the Sun. This converts it from a liquid into water vapour – a colourless gas – which then disperses into the atmosphere.

When the conditions are right, the water vapour condenses into vast numbers of tiny water droplets or ice crystals; typically, this happens when the temperature falls below a certain point. When these accumulate in sufficient quantities, clouds are formed, often where warm air rises and meets cold air.

A classification of clouds and Latin descriptions of their characteristics were first used by Luke Howard (1772–1864). There are four main categories: *stratus* (meaning layer), *cumulus* (a pile), *stratocumulus* (a layered cumulus cloud) and 'other' cloud types. These include *cirrus* (a cloud resembling a tuft) and

cumulonimbus, which is a rain-bearing cumulus cloud (*nimbus* meaning rain).

Stratus are low-lying white or grey clouds with no discernible structure. Fog is basically ground-level stratus cloud.

Stratocumulus clouds are often found near coastlines and do not usually produce much precipitation.

Cumulus clouds are short-lived structures resembling cotton wool. They occasionally produce light showers of either snow or rain.

Clouds are important components of the planet's temperature regulation process. They are extremely reflective to light; therefore, a large proportion of the sunlight that falls on them is actually bounced back into outer space. This helps to lower the amount of heat that reaches the Earth's surface and thereby plays a vital part in reducing global warming.

Coal

Coal is an organic material that has been converted into a rock-like material by geologic processes.

Coal has been an important fossil fuel for several thousand years.

There are many different types of coal. Bituminous coal, for instance, is mainly used to generate electricity in power stations, and anthracite is commonly burned to heat domestic homes.

When coal is burned, however, it releases a number of particularly harmful atmospheric pollutants. These include sooty particulates, as well as nitric oxides, sulphurous oxides and carbon dioxide.

When coal is being used in large industrial facilities, however, it is possible to use modern technology to remove some or all of these materials from the outlet flues. Particulate emissions, for example, are known to cause severe respiratory diseases, but filtration screens can remove more than 99.5 per cent of them from the exhaust fumes. Likewise, more than 90 per cent of the nitric and sulphurous oxides can be eliminated by using advanced combustion techniques.

The above methods are very expensive though, and there needs to be sufficient political support to ensure that they are employed. Many developing countries do not have the resources to use them and so continue to pollute the atmosphere at an unhealthily high rate.

See: *Environment*, page 77; *Carbon Monoxide & Carbon Dioxide*, page 40; *Nitrate Oxides*, page 135

Coastal Erosion

Coastal erosion occurs when the shoreline is damaged by a combination of the sea and the weather acting to break up or wash away those materials of which it is composed.

Over the centuries coastal erosion has had a great effect on the way the Earth looks. Especially prevalent in places where soft soils have been washed away to leave large rock formations exposed, erosion is a natural phenomenon. Today, it is considered a significant problem and great efforts are often undertaken to prevent it.

The main reason for these efforts is that humans have always been drawn to coastlines and they have always been popular places on which to build houses and other buildings. However, in recent years there have been several cases of buildings falling into the sea. Local authorities in such areas are under great pressure to prevent any loss of property.

From an environmental perspective, however, the fact that coastal erosion has accelerated in recent years is evidence of rising sea levels. This change, in fact, is the result of global warming.

In some places, it has also been increased by activities such as dredging or the close proximity of shipping to the coastline.

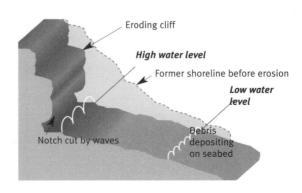

Eroding cliff

High water level

Former shoreline before erosion

Low water level

Notch cut by waves

Debris depositing on seabed

Conservation

'Conservation' is a term used to describe the deliberate efforts made by humankind to preserve animals, plants or complete habitats.

The vast majority of conservation efforts are required because of environmentally harmful activities undertaken by human beings, although there have been instances when the preservation of wildlife may be necessary due to natural events such as hurricanes or wildfires.

Cutting down forests, draining wetlands, building factories or houses, ploughing up wild places for agriculture, releasing pollutants and many other harmful processes have threatened the survival of flora and fauna.

One of the main problems is that in many parts of the world humankind's population is simply too high, leaving nowhere for the fauna and flora to exist. As a result, those species that cannot adapt either die out or their numbers become dramatically reduced.

Conservation is not restricted to the land though – well-sited marine nature reserves can be very successful too and, where overfishing is a concern, may act as valuable sanctuaries during the breeding season. While local conservation efforts form an invaluable part of the story, the most influential policies are those made at a political level. The various treaties that have more or less stopped commercial whaling are a good example of this.

See: *Endangered Species*, page 75; *Environment*, page 77; *Extinction*, page 79; *Forests*, pages 84–85; *Wetland*, page 198

Contrails

Contrails are the long white cloud-like lines that are produced in the sky by high-flying aircraft.

Most contrails are formed as the result of the condensation of moisture droplets from the exhaust gases left behind by jet engines.

Contrails can also be generated by wingtip vortices. These are fast-moving swirls of air thrown off the ends of an aircraft's wings. The changes in air pressure created can stimulate water vapour to condense. However they are formed, the condensates may then freeze into vast numbers of tiny ice crystals and leave a long, thin contrail across the sky. When the air is both humid and still, these may persist for considerable periods, but when it is dry or windy, they disperse very quickly.

There is a considerable amount of controversy over the contrails' overall environmental significance. Since they act as extra cloud cover, contrails help to reflect sunlight away from the Earth, and thus reduce the effects of global warming. On the other hand, they also act to trap heat within the atmosphere that is being radiated away from the Earth's surface, and therefore contribute to increases in global temperature.

Meteorologists have also been studying the ways in which contrails influence atmospheric chemical reactions and whether this has any impact on climate behaviour. One of the first studies was performed by NASA and known by the acronym SUCCESS, which stands for 'SUbsonic Aircraft Contrail & Clouds Effects Special Study'.

Coral Reefs

The world's coral reefs are amongst the greatest marvels to be seen in nature: most are populated by all manner of fascinating marine life.

Coral reefs are found in shallow seas, and are composed of the chalky skeletons of vast numbers of individual coral polyps (small animals that are typically only a few millimetres across and similar to tiny sea anemones).

Coral polyps have tentacles that contain numbers of dinoflagellate algae with which they have symbiotic relationships. They also use their tentacles to catch minute organisms.

In exchange for protection and certain nutrients, these microscopic organisms use photosynthesis to provide the polyps with almost all of their energy requirements. As a result of this dependence on sunlight, corals are extremely sensitive to anything that reduces the amount of light they receive. If the level of nutrients in the water rises beyond a certain point, for instance, the reefs quickly get covered with algal growths and the polyps cannot survive. Pollution, along with the unintentional release of nitrates into waterways by agriculture, are two of the main causes in the decline of reefs the world over.

Although the most famous coral reefs are found in tropical regions of the world, they are also located, to a lesser extent, in temperate waters.

See: *Environment*, page 77; *Nitrate Oxides*, page 135

Coriolis Force

In environmental terms, the expression 'Coriolis Force' is used to describe the way that the Earth's rotation causes wind streams to be deflected from their original paths.

Coriolis Force is named after a French scientist called Gaspard-Gustave Coriolis, who performed some of the first studies on it in 1835.

In simple terms, if there are no other forces acting on them, air currents usually flow in a straight line from the area of highest pressure directly towards the area of lowest pressure. Since the Earth is continually turning underneath such air masses, however, their overall path ends up curved.

The effect varies with latitude. At the equator, for instance, the force is non-existent, but as the position of any winds moves away from it, the effect increases, reaching a maximum at the poles. North of the equator, wind streams are deflected to the right, with the reverse being true in the southern hemisphere.

There are several other factors that also determine the magnitude of the force, with the speed of the winds being a major component. The Coriolis Force is responsible for the direction of rotation of atmospheric cyclones and also has a major bearing on how the world's oceanic and atmospheric currents flow. In addition, it is an important factor in astronomical physics, being responsible, among many other things, for the way in which sunspots move across the surface of the Sun.

See: *Atmosphere*, pages 22–23; *Oceans*, page 138; *Sunspots*, page 179

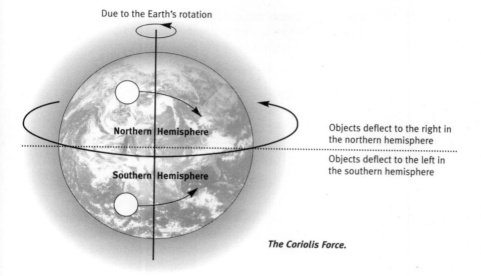

Due to the Earth's rotation

Northern Hemisphere

Southern Hemisphere

Objects deflect to the right in the northern hemisphere

Objects deflect to the left in the southern hemisphere

The Coriolis Force.

Crude Oil

Crude oil, or unprocessed oil, is a fossil fuel that is collected from underground reserves in many parts of the world.

Crude oil was formed millions of years ago from the decaying bodies of millions of tiny plants and animals that lived in ancient seas, mixed together with mud and sand.

Crude oil, also known as petroleum, contains hydrocarbons (molecules that contain hydrogen and carbon). Once crude oil has been extracted, it is transported away and refined into products like petroleum, diesel and kerosene. Consequently, most of the world's transportation systems are entirely dependent on it.

Several other very important chemicals are also derived from oil and, as a result, it has become an essential part of modern life. From an environmental perspective, however, oil and its products have exacted a heavy price since they first became widely used around 200 years ago. Many kinds of oil contain certain sulphur compounds. When these are burned, their residues are released into the atmosphere as sulphur dioxide, along with large quantities of carbon dioxide, both of which are major pollutants.

The extraction process itself can also cause widespread environmental damage, especially in vulnerable ecosystems such as those found in the Arctic. In many places, however, significant amounts of oil seep from the ground naturally, and when this occurs, the work done by the oil companies helps to reduce this source of contamination.

See: *Fossil Fuels*, pages 86–87

Crustaceans

The animals making up the sub-phylum Crustacea include such well-known creatures as crabs, lobsters, shrimp, prawns and barnacles.

Although some crustaceans live entirely on land – woodlice, for instance – the vast majority are marine. A few, such as land crabs, are terrestrial for most of their lives, but return to the sea in order to breed.

All crustaceans have hard external coverings known as exoskeletons which can vary tremendously. Some creatures, such as fish lice, have very thin shells, whereas some bigger crabs and lobsters are heavily armoured. Since exoskeletons are rigid, they need to be cast off and replaced as the animal grows.

Many members of this group are armed with claws of some description. Sometimes very powerful weapons, they are used for both defence and attack.

In all, there are about 52,000 different species of crustacean, all of which begin life as eggs that hatch into a larval stage known as a nauplius. This grows until it changes into the form that it will exist as when it becomes an adult.

Some crustaceans play a highly significant role in the regulation of the global climate. Krill, tiny, shrimp-like animals that are found in all the world's oceans, for instance, occur in such vast numbers that their swimming movements help to circulate nutrients towards the surface of the sea. This helps to sustain the organisms that live in the upper layers of the ocean and these, in turn, extract carbon dioxide from the atmosphere, thereby reducing global warming.

Cyclone

The term 'cyclone' is used in meteorology to describe a number of different atmospheric conditions, including low-pressure centres, polar cyclones, tropical cyclones and tornadoes.

The exact meaning of 'cyclone' can vary depending on who is using it and where they are from. For example, tropical cyclones are often referred to as hurricanes in North America or typhoons in Asia.

There are different types of cyclone. Low-pressure or cold-core cyclones are the zones of lowest atmospheric pressure in a given area. Typically, they are short-lived and move in a spiral fashion, centred about their focal point with the winds flowing inwards.

The Coriolis Force causes cyclones in the northern hemisphere to rotate in an anti-clockwise direction, and those in the southern hemisphere to rotate in a clockwise manner.

Tropical or warm-core cyclones are immensely powerful weather systems that develop over tropical or sub-tropical oceans, sometimes reaching over 200kph/124mph. If they reach land, they can be extremely destructive to property and livestock. Cyclones have also caused millions of deaths and serious injuries in the regions in which they strike.

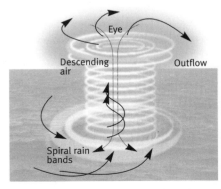

The mechanism of tropical cyclone formation.

DDT

DDT, an abbreviation of Dichloro-Diphenyl-Trichloroethane, is a man-made insecticide that first rose to prominence at the outbreak of the Second World War in 1939, primarily because of its importance in dealing with the mosquitoes that spread malaria and lice-spreading typhus.

During the first half of the 20th century, the contact poison properties of DDT were found to be effective in controlling a number of insect pests. After the end of the Second World War in 1945, DDT was in great demand, becoming a staple chemical in agriculture and horticulture. The World Health Organization (WHO) has estimated that since the end of the war the lives of approximately 25 million people have been saved through its successful application.

For many years DDT was used in large quantities but, during the 1960s, experts found that DDT was accumulating in the environment as a serious toxin and, as a consequence, was causing many problems. DDT proved especially dangerous to aquatic life, as well as to many higher predators, such as the Bald Eagle and the Peregrine Falcon, which ate the corpses of other creatures that had ingested DDT. The presence of this persistent toxin caused the numbers of these creatures to plummet, and the survival of both species was, for a while, very uncertain.

As a result of this, the use of DDT was banned in most countries, although the chemical is still used in some places to combat the vectors of such diseases as malaria and typhus.

Deforestation

Deforestation is the systematic and large-scale cutting down of trees for wood or to use the land.

O ver time, deforestation has a major impact on local conditions, affecting soil and drainage, for example, with knock-on effects for plants, animals and humans.

Humankind has practised deforestation since civilization began, but it is now destroying the world's forests at a phenomenal rate. It is estimated that 6,000 acres/24km² are being levelled during every hour of every day, and in so doing, up to 40 species of animals and plants are being made extinct.

Agricultural practices – such as the widespread slash-and-burn techniques adopted by peasant farmers and large-scale operations, supplying international markets with such products as beef or bananas – are among the causes.

The search for increased profits has also led to the use of massive quantities of artificial chemicals such as fertilizers and pesticides. Unfortunately, these chemicals poison the soil and eventually wash into waterways, weakening or killing the fauna and flora.

Commercial logging has also contributed to deforestation: vast quantities of trees are cut down for use either by the local construction industries or to sell on the international market. The world's forests are also being cleared to make way for quarrying and mining and new road and building construction. Brazil, Indonesia and Sudan are among the nations with the highest deforestation rates.

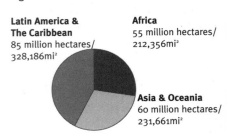

Latin America & The Caribbean
85 million hectares/ 328,186mi²

Africa
55 million hectares/ 212,356mi²

Asia & Oceania
60 million hectares/ 231,661mi²

Tropical deforestation, 1980–1995.

Desalination

Desalination is the process of removing dissolved minerals, such as salt, from sea water to make it suitable for drinking or irrigation purposes.

An energy-intensive operation that requires very expensive equipment, desalination is only done in places where fresh water is very limited. These include the small units that are found on board ships and submarines.

Worldwide, there are about 7,500 desalination plants, with about 60 per cent in the Middle East. Others are sited in North Africa, Australia, Singapore, Spain, China and the drier parts of the United States.

There are several different ways to perform the process, including various forms of distillation, forward and reverse osmosis, evaporation–condensation, and many others.

Desalination is environmentally significant, primarily because it makes agriculture and human habitation possible where it would otherwise not be. This often results in native plants and animals being displaced and fragile habitats destroyed.

The processing plants are usually built next to the sea on ecologically valuable land and also have deleterious impacts on the marine life in their immediate proximities. One of the biggest concerns is how to dispose of by-products – liquid wastes containing high salt concentrations, chemicals and even toxic metals. These are often discharged directly into the sea, with potentially hazardous consequences for marine life.

Deserts

Deserts are places that are defined as having less than 254mm/10in of precipitation annually, and that the evaporation rates they display exceed this amount.

About one-fifth of the planet is covered by deserts. Although they are typically associated with very hot climates and regions, cold deserts also exist. Other types include semi-arid and coastal deserts.

The largest desert in the world is located inside inner Antarctica, where the air in the surrounding areas is so cold that any water vapour is instantly frozen before any moisture can reach it. With a total area of around 14.2 million km²/5.5 million mi², it far exceeds the size of the biggest hot desert – the Sahara (which measures 9 million km²/3.5 million mi²).

The driest hot deserts receive less than 2.5 mm/0.1 in of rain every year and cover around 12 per cent of the Earth's surface. The organisms that live in deserts are very sensitive to environmental changes. This is because the adaptations that they have had to make in order to be able to survive in the extreme conditions are so specialized that they cannot live in any other way. It is therefore vital that deserts are protected from human exploitation.

Large mammals do not typically exist in deserts. Examples of animals often found in these areas include burrowing nocturnal carnivores (such as badgers and coyotes), insects, reptiles (such as lizards and snakes) and birds like the Burrowing Owl (in semi-arid deserts) or the Bald Eagle (in coastal desert regions).

Dioxins

The name 'dioxin' is applied to a group of chemicals that are known as polychlorinated dibenzodioxins.

Dioxins are of great environmental concern as they can build up in plants and animals, including humans, as well as the soil. The long-term effects of the various dioxins are still not fully understood, but it is thought that many are carcinogenic and that there is no safe level of exposure.

Almost everyone has measurable quantities of dioxins inside them, with the majority coming from the food they consume. Fish, meat and dairy products provide the main sources of human dioxin contamination.

Exposure can, however, come from a variety of other sources, including some types of pesticides and herbicides, the exhaust fumes from diesel engines and the burning of certain types of wood.

Industrial incinerators are the biggest contributors of atmospheric dioxins, with chemical and fertilizer manufacturing plants, steel mills and coal-fired power stations following closely, along with bleaching plants in paper mills and certain plastics factories. There are a few natural sources, too, which include volcanoes and forest fires.

The authorities in most developed countries have regulations that control the way in which dioxins may be used, although monitoring is not always as thorough as it should be.

See: *Carcinogens*, page 41; *Fishing*, page 80; *Pesticides*, pages 147

Dredging

Dredging is the process of removing sediments from the beds of lakes, rivers, estuaries or the sea.

The process of dredging is usually performed using a device that is dropped into the water and dragged along until it is full up with spoil, whereupon it is hauled to the surface and emptied.

Dredging can be done from the shore or from a boat. There are many reasons for dredging a waterway, the main one being to keep it navigable for use by shipping. Another common reason is to obtain construction materials from gravel beds.

Unfortunately, dredging can cause a number of environmental problems. These include stirring up huge quantities of mud and silt, which can hang in suspension for a long time before settling, and so blocking out the light. This can kill animals and plants that are totally dependent on sunlight for their survival.

Disturbing the sediments also releases into the environment any toxic chemicals that have settled there, such as anti-fouling agents like tributyltin, as well as oil residues, PCBs, and heavy metals such as mercury. Other problems caused by dredging are noise disturbance, overspill of sediments and a small amount of light pollution during operations conducted at night.

In the developed world the dredging industry takes its environmental responsibilities very seriously. In the United Kingdom, for example, dredging is regulated by the government, and licences are issued to enable organizations to dredge in particular areas. This is not necessarily the case, however, in some developing nations, where serious damage is done on a daily basis via unregulated, unlicenced and therefore indiscriminate dredging activity.

Drought

Droughts are defined as abnormally dry periods that are severe enough to cause 'serious hydrologic imbalance in the affected area'.

To a certain degree, droughts are a normal feature of the world's variable weather systems, although they can also be created by human activity, or made worse by them.

In the 1930s, for example, poor farming techniques contributed to the severity of the droughts that occurred on the Great Plains of the United States. This was a time of severe hardship for millions of Americans, and around 20 million hectares/50 million acres of the region dried out to such an extent that they became known as the 'Dust Bowls'.

If a drought lasts for too long, an area's vegetation may not be able to recover, and the region may turn into a desert. When this happens, it can be a catastrophe for humans as well as for the local fauna and flora.

Sometimes droughts are caused by events that happen a long way away from the places in which they occur. For instance, if there happens to be a shortage of snow on a mountain range, the lack of melt waters in the spring may cause local rivers to run dry, and could therefore result in droughts further on downstream.

Dust Storms

Dust storms occur across the world in areas where a combination of arid climates and high winds can be found.

Sand storms are essentially the same thing as dust storms, although the airborne particles are somewhat larger.

Dust storms usually start when hot air forms updrafts close to the ground. This causes winds to blow in from the sides, and when these are strong enough, they displace loose surface material and transport it into the updraft, whereupon it is carried high into the air. This often happens as the result of the strong winds created by thunderstorms.

The material that is lifted eventually returns to the ground and may be deposited many thousands of miles away. In severe storms, seemingly solid walls of dust or sand form and these can be as much as 1,525m/5,000ft high. The actual height reached is determined by a combination of the atmospheric conditions and the weight of the debris.

Such events can cause whole areas to be denuded of all soil cover, leaving behind a vista of bare rock. It can also result in other locations being buried under thousands of tons of debris. Either way, it can lead to loss of livelihoods and severe hardship.

Earthquakes

Earthquakes are caused by movements in the tectonic plates which make up the Earth's crust. They can range from barely detectable to catastrophic.

Many of the mountain ranges, rivers and seas that we know today are the result of earthquakes.

There are, on average, about 35 earthquakes each day. Some regions experience very few if any, whereas others lying in active geological zones, such as California and Japan, are hit by them frequently.

One of the most famous areas lies along the San Andreas fault, near San Francisco, California. This region has suffered many serious earthquakes. The last major one occurred in 1906, killing an estimated 3,000 people and leaving around 300,000 homeless. Measurements have shown that stress levels within the fault have now built up to the point where another event is likely to happen at any time.

Earthquake activity is measured across the world by seismic recording stations, of which there are about 4,000 in total. As time goes by and more is learned about the science, there are hopes that before long it will be possible to predict more accurately when a major event is going to occur.

Ecology

*The word 'ecology' has its roots in the Greek words
'oikos' (household) and 'logos' (knowledge).*

Ecology is the study of ecosystems,
their composition and how the
various components interact with
one another.

The discipline of ecology brings together
a great number of specializations in
order to understand the way in which a
particular environment functions.

These start at the molecular level
with biochemists examining protein
structures, for example, and then
grow in scale, bringing in geneticists,
cell biologists and those who study
entire organisms. These include
behaviourists, zoologists, botanists,
and many others, and beyond this,

there are people who study systems,
such as meteorology, agriculture,
forestry and geology.

By understanding all these factors,
it is possible to determine the well-
being of an ecosystem from a holistic
perspective and pinpoint any specific
threats it faces. Consequently, any
measures that may need to be taken to
protect it can be easily identified.

By monitoring the ecology of various
regions, it is therefore possible to assess
the likely long-term effects of factors like
climate change, and in particular, the
significance of global warming and the
after-effects of natural disasters such
as hurricanes and volcanic eruptions.

See: *Agriculture*, page 9; *Climate*, pages 50–51; *Global Warming,
pages 96–97; Organism*, page 141

Electric Lighting

For more than 100 years, electric lighting has been an integral part of the lives of most people in the developed world.

While electric lighting is relatively cheap and works well, from an environmental perspective it is not particularly energy efficient.

Technological innovations have resulted in a number of solutions to overcome this problem, including fluorescent bulbs that last up to 10 times longer and use less energy than the old incandescent equivalents.

Although such measures are important, one of the most significant issues concerns the developing world, where about 1.5 billion people rely on kerosene lamps for all their lighting.

This produces dangerous indoor pollution though, and it is thought that the diseases caused by its smoke are responsible for about 1.5 million deaths every year.

One way around this is to replace such lighting with solar-powered LED lamps. Once the initial purchase cost has been met, these are not only free to use, but produce much more light. This concept is potentially one of the most immediate ways to improve people's lives and the health of the environment. Consequently, many governments and charities have started distributing LED lamps in developing regions.

See: *Solar Power*, page 172–173

El Niño

'El Niño' is the term used for a short-lived warm oceanic current that develops annually along the coast of Ecuador and Peru around Christmas time.

El Niño usually only lasts a few weeks, but every few years or so it lasts a great deal longer – from several months to a year at a time.

The warm water that El Niño carries unbalances nutrient-rich seas, and the local fishing industries can collapse.

There can also be far-reaching consequences for the atmosphere, such as an increase in the number of tropical storms in the eastern Pacific area, but a reduction in the Atlantic, Gulf of Mexico and the Caribbean Sea regions.

Elsewhere the weather can also be changed, bringing droughts across the southern hemisphere, from Africa to India, Australasia, and South America. The vast wildernesses of Antarctica are also affected, with the amount of sea ice increasing in El Niño years.

Experts have still to establish a direct link between such events, although some believe that the wind shear, which is induced by unusually warm oceanic currents, disrupts tropical storms and prevents them from developing into hurricanes.

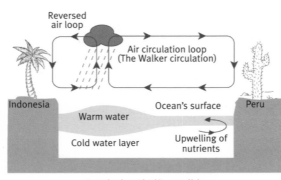

Developing El Niño conditions.

Endangered Species

An endangered species is an organism that is under threat of extinction.

The term 'endangered species' can apply equally to plants and animals, as well as to subspecies.

In modern times, the vast majority of threats to the survival of the species of flora or fauna are the result of humankind's activities. Habitat loss is by far the most common cause, but there are other factors that can lower a population to critical levels. These include environmental pollution, industrial accidents and over-exploitation through such practices as fishing.

Experts believe that well over a third of all plants and animals are endangered to some degree, although the situation is actually worse than this since, in some instances, the species concerned support others and therefore their survival or demise is important to that of other species too.

Conservationists are making strenuous efforts to improve matters, but in reality they can only cope with a small number of the issues needing to be addressed. Although it is sometimes possible to persuade governments to pass laws protecting certain species, in some parts of the world there are insufficient resources to enforce them.

Examples of species that are in danger of becoming extinct are the panda, polar bear, Bengal Tiger, orang-utan, Asian Elephant and rhinoceros.

See: *Animal Kingdom*, page 17; *Extinction*, page 79; *Fishing*, page 80; *Plants*, page 150

Energy Conservation

Almost all forms of human-made devices rely on artificial sources of energy at some time in their manufacture or use.

Over the years, humankind has become very reliant on artificial sources of energy. Such dependence is wasteful, since it both consumes resources and generates pollution. There is an increasing need to minimize waste by looking after the Earth's resources much more carefully.

This policy is known as 'energy conservation', and is something that everyone can do, starting with the simplest of actions such as switching off unnecessary lights and not leaving electrical equipment on standby.

On a larger scale, the efficiency of industrial machinery can often be significantly improved, although this can require substantial capital investment. While some economies are strong enough to sustain such actions, many are not, especially those in developing countries.

One of the most cost-effective means of conserving energy can be achieved by fitting thermal insulation to buildings. This not only cuts down on the amount of heating fuel used, but also reduces emissions and, in the long-term, can save money as well.

Working from home is also good for the environment, as it lowers the number of journeys made; this saves fuel, minimizes pollution, and reduces road congestion.

Energy conservation also goes hand-in-hand with utilizing energy from renewable sources, such as the Sun, wind or waves, as opposed to relying on fossil fuels, for example, which are non-renewable sources of energy.

Environment

The word 'environment' describes the ecosystem of a given area – be this on a local, national or global scale.

Inherent within the word 'environment' are all the factors that influence it, from geology to the fauna and flora, as well as the prevailing climate.

In modern times, the environment refers to the entire global system. That is, everything from the outermost reaches of the atmosphere to the Earth's inner core. Inherent within this are all the factors that influence the environment, from its geology to the fauna and flora as well as the prevailing climate.

The expression 'environmentalism' refers to a movement to protect, nurture and restore the world's natural places. It seeks to conserve resources and minimize the harmful effects of humankind's activities. This means reducing pollution levels and the haphazard dumping of waste materials, as well as managing any factors that contribute to climate change.

Concern for the environment has been expressed since the Industrial Revolution (c. 1750–1850), although no-one took it seriously then. It took the demise of the Passenger Pigeon, once North America's most common bird, and the near extinction of the American Bison, for people to take notice.

These days there are many different forms of environmentalism. Some focus on issues such as the preservation of indigenous cultures or stopping commercial whaling. World-famous organizations, such as Greenpeace, have focused people's attention (and also that of governments) on environmental issues such as global warming, deforestation, over-fishing, the misuse of natural resources and pollution.

See: *Deforestation*, page 64; *Fishing*, page 80; *Global Warming*, pages 96–97

E-Waste

*E-waste describes any waste that derives
from discarded electronic appliances.*

Electronic appliances can range from
such items as mobile phones and
computers to domestic washing
machines and refrigerators.

E-waste also includes the parts of any
commercial or industrial machines
that contain electronic circuitry. Most
of the components used in these
devices contain one or more toxic or
carcinogenic substances and typically
include such materials as lead,
cadmium and mercury, as well as
polychlorinated biphenyls (PCBs).

While these substances are
particularly harmful to the environment,
they also have a significant commercial
value if they are efficiently recovered.
In recent years, many countries have
passed strict laws regarding the disposal
of e-waste, although this has often led
to large shipments of old electrical
equipment being transported to such
countries as China.

In such places, the laws on material
recovery are very lax. Unfortunately this
has resulted in large numbers of back-
street operations using the most basic
of techniques. Typically, there is little
in the way of safety equipment for the
protection of the workers and highly
toxic materials are burned openly with
no concern whatsoever for either the
environment or human health.

See: *Environment*, page 77

Extinction

The term 'extinction' is used when a species of animal or plant dies out. Extinction usually occurs when the death rate exceeds the birth rate of a species.

The death of a given species of plant or animal may be local or national, in which case the species concerned is described as having died out in a particular area or country. On the other hand, the extinction may be total, whereby the organism ceases to exist as a living entity.

Although humankind is responsible for the loss of countless species, extinctions have occurred ever since the first life forms evolved. One of the better known examples is known as the 'Cretaceous–Tertiary extinction'. This happened about 65-million years ago when, it is believed, either a large asteroid hit the Earth or a series of large volcanic eruptions took place. Around this time the majority of large life forms, such as the dinosaurs, died out and popular belief is that the events are somehow linked.

At between 100 and 1,000 times the background level (ie: the level normally expected without humankind's interference), the rate of extinctions is currently higher than it has ever been. Humankind can take the blame for almost all of these losses and the destruction of rainforests, one of the most diverse habitats on the planet, is a contributory factor. Examples of species that are now extinct include the dodo, quagga, the Tasmanian Tiger and Baiji white dolphin.

See: *Endangered Species*, page 75

Fishing

Humankind has caught and eaten fish since ancient times, and has devised increasingly efficient ways of doing so ever since.

The global population has now reached the point where demand for fish far outstrips supply. This has resulted in many of the world's largest fish stocks, including cod, being so heavily over-fished that they have been more or less wiped out.

The herring fisheries of the North Sea were once one of the biggest of their kind and the industry supported many thousands of people. A complete lack of regulation and over-fishing, however, led to so many fish being caught that the fish populations were unable to sustain themselves and they crashed during the late 1970s and early 1980s.

Similar situations have occurred all over the world – the Newfoundland, Canada, cod fishery collapsed in 1992 after years of over-exploitation and the Peruvian anchovy fishery also failed for similar reasons in the 1970s.

As a result of the demise of certain fish species, various regulations have been imposed across the world. Some place strict limits on the numbers, sizes and species of fish that can be caught. Others have set aside specific areas, such as marine reserves, to provide safe zones in which the fish can breed.

Some, but by no means all, of these measures have been successful. However, as more is learned about the ecology of the marine environment, people can make better-informed decisions about it.

Many fishing methods result in the unintentional deaths of other animals. These include dolphins caught in trawl nets and albatrosses hooked and drowned by longlines.

Flooding

Floods have been a feature of the world's weather systems since well before life first evolved.

Flooding results from large quantities of water being released into an area at a rate that is greater than the ability of the natural run-off and evaporation processes to disperse. This is not helped by humankind's determination to build houses on flood plains and, in so doing, concreting over most of the natural soakaways.

The floodwater concerned may be from intense rainfall, or it may have come from many miles away via rivers or canals. Where this happens suddenly and with no warning, the events are referred to as 'flash floods'. These are by far the most dangerous kinds of flooding, and many people the world over lose their lives to them every year.

Although floods can cause enormous amounts of damage to both property and livelihoods, they can also bring benefits. This is because flood waters typically carry huge amounts of nutrient-rich mud and silt in suspension. When the area dries out, this is left behind and acts as a valuable natural fertilizer.

As a result, many farming communities have been deliberately established on flood plains. Examples of these include the ancient civilizations of the rivers Nile, Euphrates and Indus. These settlements thrived for many thousands of years.

See: *El Niño*, page 74

Food Chain

A food chain is a common method of expressing the way that the organisms in a particular ecosystem feed on each other.

Food chains usually start with the lowest species at the bottom. Typically, these are plants or minute creatures such as plankton.

The chain then works up through successive layers until the highest predators are reached. A simple example could start with a field of grass on which caterpillars feed. These are then eaten by song birds, which are, in turn, consumed by birds of prey. The same principle applies to marine environments too, in which phytoplankton at the lowest level are eaten by small fish. These tiny animals are devoured by larger fish, that are, in their turn, preyed upon by still bigger ones. These larger predators are then caught and eaten by humans and the cycle is endlessly repeated.

An example of such a chain would be as follows:

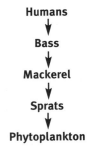

Humans
↓
Bass
↓
Mackerel
↓
Sprats
↓
Phytoplankton

Although food chains can be a good way of representing the order of predation in an ecosystem, they are overly simplistic, as the interplay between members is actually far more complex. A more accurate scenario can be depicted by the use of a food web, where all known relationships can be clearly shown.

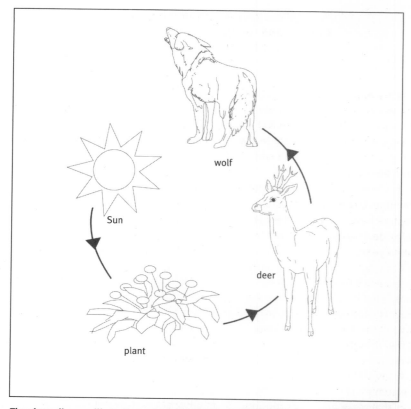

The above diagram illustrates a simple food chain. Sunlight (left) is the power source for the Earth, triggering photosynthesis in plants (bottom). Animals, such as the deer (right), eat the plants, and in turn are consumed by predators, such as the wolf (top).

Forests

Forests are ecosystems dominated by trees and woody vegetation such as shrubs, vines and plants.

Forests are home to two-thirds of all plant and animal species found on Earth and are central to the survival of millions of people. They are vital to the survival of the planet. The Earth was once far more covered by ancient forests, but illegal logging, industrial-scale farming, climate change and other factors have led to about 80 per cent being destroyed or degraded in the last 30 years.

There are many types of forest and these are found in cold, temperate, sub-tropical or tropical regions. They cover vast parts of the world, from lowland areas up to the edge of the tree line at high altitudes.

The climates of forests range from arid at one extreme to monsoon at the other. The trees that make up forests can vary tremendously. At high latitudes, for instance, they may be dominated by a single species – typically a birch or a conifer, for example.

In the rainforests, however, there may be hundreds of different kinds of trees. In temperate and cold climates, many of these are deciduous, meaning that they shed their leaves before winter, and then grow them again in the spring.

Forests are incredibly important places as far as the environment is concerned. They not only act as homes to a vast number of animals, plants and fungi, but also play a vital role in the atmospheric and hydrologic systems.

In the latter part of the 20th century, experts became increasingly concerned with the deforestation of the planet. Today, about 25 to 30 per cent of greenhouse gases released into the atmosphere each year are the product of deforestation.

Forests all over the world are now under threat from logging and other environmental damage.

Fossil Fuels

Fossil fuels are substances that are derived from ancient sources and burned to produce some kind of power.

The most common types of fossil fuels are coal and oil, both of which were formed many millions of years ago as the result of the fossilization of plant matter. When these materials are refined and later burned as fuel, they release large quantities of carbon into the atmosphere. This can be in several different forms, ranging from gases such as carbon monoxide and carbon dioxide to fine particulates like fly ash.

The release of harmful pollutants is not the only contentious issue regarding the use of fossil fuels, however. The main problem is that, although they are cheap to extract and refine, their supply is finite and is rapidly running out.

Consequently, they have risen in value, and have begun to dominate many aspects of global politics and various military conflicts have been fought over gas and oil reserves. These include several bitter actions during the Second World War (1939–1945) in the Caucases, Egypt and the Far East.

It is currently thought that there is enough oil to last about 35 more years, sufficient natural gas for about 55 more years, and coal stocks that could last for around 250 years. These figures are based on our present rate of consumption, though, and do not take into account the way in which the economies of such countries as China and India will change over the next few decades. It is entirely possible that they will expand far faster than has been predicted; if their populations were to acquire a similar number of motor vehicles to those possessed by western countries, the increased rate of consumption would cause the world supply of fossil fuels to collapse in a matter of a few years. There is therefore an urgent need to find alternative sources of fuel that are not harmful to the environment.

The above picture shows the by-product of burning fossil fuels on an industrial scale.

Fujita–Pearson Tornado Scale

The Fujita–Pearson Tornado Scale is a means of measuring the power of tornadoes.

This scale was devised by Tetsuya Fujita of the University of Chicago and Allen Pearson of the National Severe Storms Forecast Center.

When measuring a tornado's power, the position on the scale is determined by visually assessing the damage done after it has passed by. This includes examining any damage to property or trees to help establish the tornado's path, width and length. The weakest level is F0; the strongest level is F5.

The Fujita–Pearson Tornado Scale	Speed (mph)	Strength	Path length (miles)	Width (yards)	Damage
F0 – Gale Tornado	40–72	Weak	0.3–0.9	6–17	Light damage to property and small trees.
F1 – Moderate Tornado	73–112	Moderate	1.0–3.1	18–55	Moderate damage to property, cars pushed off the road.
F2 – Significant Tornado	113–157	Strong	3.2–9.9	56–175	Major damage to property and large trees.
F3 – Severe Tornado	158–206	Severe	10–31	176–566	Severe damage to property and large trees uprooted.
F4 – Devastating Tornado	207–260	Very serious	32–99	528–1584	Houses destroyed, cars thrown through the air.
F5 – Incredible Tornado	261–318	Extreme	100–315	1760–5456	Entire houses destroyed, cars thrown 100 yards or more.

Gaia Hypothesis

The Gaia Hypothesis suggests that all the various components making up the Earth should be viewed together as a functional system that acts in the manner of a single life form.

Named after Gaia, the Greek goddess of the Earth, and proposed by Professor James Lovelock while he was working as a scientist for NASA in the 1960s, the hypothesis says that Earth should be viewed as one entity rather than as a number of individual components, such as plants, animals, weather systems, geology, and so on.

The Gaia Hypothesis postulates that Earth is a self-regulating mechanism, and that when one part changes, the others within it act in such a way that stability is regained.

Since the hypothesis was first proposed, it has been the subject of vigorous debate with a high media profile. Many experts rejected it although its proponents claimed to have examined it via rigorous scientific methods, and in passing various tests it proved its validity. Consequently, it is often also referred to as the 'Gaia Theory' (a theory being a proven hypothesis).

Nowadays, the concept is usually termed 'Earth System Science', and under this label is more widely accepted. In recent years, Professor Lovelock has also been on record in claiming that the phenomenon of global warming is the response of an 'outraged planet'.

See: *Global Warming*, pages 96–97

Genetic Diversity

The expression 'genetic diversity' is used to describe any variation in genes, nucleotides, chromosomes or whole genomes of organisms.

Many experts state a species' chance of survival over extended periods of time increases with diversity.

Experts believe this is because gene variation is reflected as either physical or behavioural differences between individuals. Some of these characteristics are inherently better at adapting to and coping with particular changes than others. Natural selection then takes over, removing any individuals that are unable to survive, leaving a population that is better suited to its new situation.

One of the problems that endangered species have is that their low populations often have insufficient gene variability for the surviving individuals to cope with changes in circumstance. These may include disease, habitat loss, pollution and so on.

An example of genetic modification to circumstances might be the hypothetical situation of a group of tortoises on a desert island. In times of drought, all the small plants die out, leaving behind only shrubs and trees. Consequently, only the tortoises that have long necks can reach the food, and all the others perish. As a result, the genes that provide long necks are then inherited by subsequent generations and this characteristic will become more common among them. In order to retain diversity, however, nature will ensure that some creatures will still have short or medium-length necks.

Genetically Modified Organisms

*Genetically modified organisms are
plants or animals that have resulted from some
form of synthetic gene manipulation.*

The term 'genetically modified' indicates the use of recombinant DNA techniques (procedures to join together, or recombine, segments of DNA) whereby the genetic information from one kind of animal or plant is incorporated into the fundamental make-up of another.

Genetic modification can create, for instance, crops with resistance to herbicides or cattle that produce better-quality milk. Before these techniques became possible, genetic manipulation was performed by selective cross-breeding, in which individuals with desirable attributes were bred with one another. The offspring were carefully chosen to propagate these characteristics, and bred again until the desired outcome was achieved.

Such traditional methods are still in use across the world, although they are extremely limited in comparison with synthetic gene manipulation.

Although the use of recombinant DNA techniques theoretically allows for an almost infinite range of genetic variations to be tried out, this is not necessarily a good thing.

There is currently a lot of pressure to delay the introduction of genetically modified organisms into the natural world. This is because of concerns that they will interbreed with similar species – ultimately wiping them out – or because they may mutate into forms that are harmful to the environment.

Geoengineering

Geoengineering is based on the idea that humankind can in some way artificially modify the Earth's environment to achieve certain aims, such as preventing global warming.

Although geoengineering is a relatively new concept, there are various interpretations as to exactly what it means. Overall, though, it generally seeks to improve human living conditions.

Many of the leading proposals relating to this concept are aimed at reversing the effects of global warming. One idea, for instance, put forward by leading scientists James Lovelock, who developed the Gaia Hypothesis, and Chris Rapley, the director of the Science Museum in London, suggests that large pipes could be used to bring nutrient-rich water from the deep oceans to the surface. This, scientists argue, would foster vast populations of plankton, which, in turn, would absorb enormous quantities of carbon dioxide from the atmosphere. Since carbon dioxide is one of the primary greenhouse gases, this action could possibly help to reduce climate change.

Whether Lovelock and Rapley's idea could actually be put into practice is not yet clear. It would require thousands or even millions of the devices, and their potential efficacy is unknown. The idea is not without merit though, and at the very least should stimulate further debate and research into the subject.

See: *Climate,* pages 50–51; *Gaia Hypothesis*, page 89; *Global Warming*, pages 96–97

Geothermal Energy

Geothermal energy is derived from heat sourced from within the Earth's surface.

Geothermal energy can be used to power domestic or industrial heating systems, or alternatively to drive electricity generators.

There are many ways in which this heat can be accessed. In some regions, for instance, there are natural steam vents, which are relatively simple to harness. In others, however, it is necessary to drill deep bore holes and then pump water through them to heat it.

Another method of extracting heat energy from below the surface is to use devices that are known as ground source heat pumps. These exploit the natural difference between the temperatures of the air and the subsoil to power heating systems.

Although geothermal energy systems still require manufacture and transportation to where they will be based, they are better for the environment than those that depend on fossil fuels. They are, however, usually expensive to install, and despite low operating costs, require significant up-front capital outlay.

As conventional methods of heating continue to get more expensive, though, geothermal energy is becoming far more popular, and is likely to continue to do so for many years to come, as more and more people recognize its advantages.

Glaciers

*Glaciers are large bodies of ice that have formed
as the result of the accumulation of many hundreds
or even thousands of years of snowfall.*

———

**The rate at which snow builds up
depends on how much of it melts
during the summer. As it gradually gets
thicker, it becomes heavier and heavier,
until the layers at the bottom become
compressed into ice.**

When there is sufficient weight behind it,
the ice will begin flowing. Where it is
relatively thin, the pressures involved are
low and, as a result, it moves very slowly,
and can even appear to be immobile.

Where the ice has built up to
substantial thicknesses, however, it can
travel several metres a day.

Glaciers begin to form when snow
and ice accumulate in permanent layers
over many years, and do not generally
begin moving until they are at least
50m/164ft thick.

This is because the friction that holds
the ice to the ground below is so strong
that massive forces are needed to
overcome it. When these build up to a
sufficient level, a process called 'plastic
deformation' takes place, and the ice flows
away from the point of greatest pressure.

Glaciers currently cover about 10
per cent of the world's surface, but with
the onset of global warming, many of
them are melting at an unprecedented
rate. This is releasing vast quantities of
water and contributing to the problem
of rising sea levels.

See: *Sea Level*, page 167

Global Dimming

Global dimming is an environmental issue that results from the reduction in the amount of sunlight that reaches the Earth's surface, due to the presence of vast numbers of small particles which block it out.

There are many different schools of thought on the causes and implications of global dimming, but generally it is agreed by experts that, between 1960 and 1990, the amount of light getting through the Earth's surface declined by four per cent.

Since 1990 this figure has once again been on the rise. The majority of the atmospheric particulates that contribute to global dimming are in the form of microscopic pieces of soot. These are either produced by natural sources, such as volcanoes and wildfires, or by humankind's activities.

These include a variety of industrial processes, as well as the exhaust fumes of cars, trucks and aircraft.

It is thought that global dimming directly interferes with the natural cycle of precipitation, evaporation, condensation and re-precipitation and that droughts have occurred across the world because of this.

So far, however, scientists are still trying to discover how it is possible to have global dimming and global warming occurring at the same time, and a great deal of research into this intriguing phenomenon is still needed to establish the real picture.

Global Warming

*The term 'global warming' refers to the way in which
the Earth's average temperature is rising with
devastating effect to the climate and environment.*

I n recent years, scientists have
become increasingly concerned about
the greenhouse effect – that is, the
impact that greenhouse gases (any gas
that absorbs infrared radiation in the
atmosphere) have had in making the
Earth warmer by trapping energy in the
atmosphere. This global warming will
have long-lasting effects on the world.

In the last 100 years alone, the surface
temperature of the Earth has gone up
by about 10°F (about 5°C). The rate of
change seems to be increasing, with the
10 warmest years of the 20th century
all occurring between 1985 and 2000.
Although global warming has occurred
in the past, it is widely thought that
industrial activity underlies much of
the present trend.

The causes of global warming,
however, are extremely complex, and few
scientists are in complete agreement on
the issue. For instance, no-one knows
exactly what influence the world's fauna
and flora have on the atmosphere. The
Sun also produces variable amounts of
solar radiation, and this can have a
marked effect on the amount of heat
the Earth receives.

Whatever the causal mechanisms are,
the result is that snowfields, glaciers
and vast areas of pack ice have melted,
causing sea levels to rise between
10cm/4in and 20cm/8in in the last
century. If the trend continues, many
low-lying areas will become permanently
flooded before very long. Countries
such as Bangladesh are suffering
from increased flooding due to climatic
change. These threats have generated
a huge amount of concern all the way
from the general public up to the highest
levels of government.

In the United Kingdom, for example,
an official report called the *Stern Review*

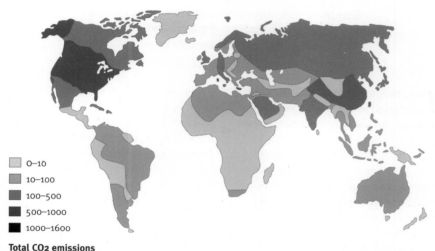

Carbon emissions around the world.

- 0–10
- 10–100
- 100–500
- 500–1000
- 1000–1600

**Total CO₂ emissions
(million metric tons carbon)**

was published on 30 October 2006. Led by Nicholas Stern, a senior economist and government advisor, it was the largest review on the subject ever conducted. It basically states that unless severe measures are taken, climate change could cause massive economic failures, and widespread hardship. Despite the breadth and depth of its coverage, the report has been heavily criticized, especially for the justifications it makes for increased taxation.

See: *Fossil Fuels,* pages 86–87; *Greenhouse Effect,* page 99

Grasslands

Grasslands, or savannahs, steppes, pampas and prairies, are areas that are predominantly populated with grasses of one kind or another.

The species that make up grasslands vary considerably, based on the type of biome and also environmental factors.

About one-quarter of the Earth's land is covered by grassland, ranging from polar tundras and temperate and alpine areas to those found in tropical and subtropical regions.

Grasslands are known by many different names. They are called savannahs in Africa, rangelands (Australia), steppes (Eurasia), pampas (South America) and prairies (North America). Despite sharing common characteristics, each grassland differs slightly. For example, steppes receive little rainfall and have low grass, while savannahs are wetter with long grass.

The underlying soil chemistry is a major component in their make-up – for example, calcareous soils, such as those found where chalk is prevalent, are populated by grasses that are very different from those where there is a high peat content.

The animals that graze them also have a great deal of influence on the types of grasses that are able to survive. Rabbits and sheep produce a very short turf, whereas the presence of cows results in much longer, lush meadows. Sadly, many of world's larger grasslands have been ploughed up for agricultural use. Historically, much of the American Midwest was covered by natural grasslands but this has been replaced by such crops as wheat and barley.

See: *Savannahs,* page 165; *Steppe,* page 174

Greenhouse Effect

The term the 'greenhouse effect' describes the way in which the atmosphere acts to raise the planet's overall temperature.

This term derives from the fact that when sunlight shines into a greenhouse, it is converted into heat in a form that cannot easily radiate back out again. The temperature inside is therefore much higher than that outside. In much the same way, the atmosphere traps heat and the extent to which it does this is determined by its exact make-up. Certain gases trap more heat than others, and these are termed 'greenhouse gases'. Examples include carbon dioxide, methane and various chloroflurocarbons.

By far the most influential component in the greenhouse effect, however, is water vapour. This is responsible for about 60 per cent of the greenhouse effect, while carbon dioxide – the most widely publicized 'culprit' – only contributes about 20 per cent. As global temperatures rise, the rate of evaporation of water increases, and so more heat is trapped within the atmosphere. On the other hand, this water vapour then forms clouds, shielding the Earth from the Sun's heat, thereby reducing the effects of global warming.

Quite how this affects the global climate remains a matter of some debate in scientific circles. Currently, the atmosphere ensures that the average temperature of the Earth's surface is about 33°C/91°F warmer than it would be if the greenhouse effect did not exist. So, life as we know it would therefore not be possible.

Greenpeace

Formed in 1971, the organization Greenpeace promotes, fosters and takes part in a range of environmentally related issues and activities.

Greenpeace aims to 'ensure the ability of the Earth to nurture life in all its diversity'. In the early days, the organization was best known for its efforts to stop commercial whaling. Since then, however, it has developed a much wider focus.

Greenpeace has a large number of offices and several laboratories located around the world. This network is paid for by around three million supporters, as well as through grants from various charitable trusts.

Over the years, the organization has taken part in many controversial activities. These include attempts to prevent whaling, interfering with the oil industry and closing down automobile production lines.

It has campaigned on issues such as the prevention of over-fishing, the exposure of illegal toxic waste dumping, the poor management of nuclear and industrial facilities and the protection of important habitats.

These actions have made the organization very unpopular in many political and business circles. This is best illustrated by the events of 1985 when its flagship the *Rainbow Warrior* was blown up by French secret service agents after it interfered with their nuclear weapons testing programme in the Pacific Ocean.

Aside from direct action, Greenpeace also lobbies tirelessly for the creation of nature reserves, both on land and at sea. It is committed to stopping both climate change and the use of toxic materials and, in addition, actively seeks to promote peace and total nuclear disarmament throughout the world.

Gulf Stream

The Gulf Stream is a large, warm oceanic current that circulates in the northern Atlantic Ocean.

One of the strongest of its kind, the Gulf Stream has major environmental significance. It has a direct influence on the climates of North America and Europe, and many of the countries that border the North Atlantic have much milder climates than they would if it did not exist. The average temperature of the British Isles, for instance, is about 9°C/48°F higher than that of other countries on the same latitude.

The Gulf Stream arises because of the movements in the Atlantic North Equatorial Current which flows from North West Africa across to the northeastern coast of South America.

This then moves northwards, creating the Gulf Stream, which begins in the Gulf of Mexico, and then passes through the Strait of Florida before travelling up the northern coast of North America.

It typically flows at about four knots at the surface, and reaches to depths of between 800m/2.624ft and 1200m/3,937ft. As the water moves northwards, it loses heat thanks to contact with cold winds and evaporative cooling. This results in colder, heavier and saltier water which, by the time it has reached the polar region, has sunk well below that of the surface zone. This then flows southwards again, completing the cycle that began off the coast of North Africa.

Hail

Hail is a type of precipitation that is composed of frozen raindrops.

Hail is created in storm clouds when both snowflakes and rain are being formed at the same time.

As snowflakes grow in size, water droplets start sticking to them and freeze, forming a lump of ice. The increased weight causes this to fall towards the base of the cloud. Many ice particles get caught in strong updrafts and are carried back to the top of the cloud where they are covered water droplets, and the cycle begins over again.

The only limit to the size of the hailstones produced is the strength of the updrafts. When the updrafts do not have sufficient strength to lift the particles any more, they fall as hail.

Small hailstones are rarely anything more than a nuisance, but large stones are different. In May 1996, for example, large hailstones killed around 100 people in China and destroyed 35,000 homes. In the United States, hail comes second only to hurricanes in the amount of agricultural damage caused by weather conditions.

Hail formation.

Hail growing in circulating convection currents

Hail now too large to hold in cloud, falling to earth causing strong downdraught

Freezing level

Raindrops being sucked into the updraught

Habitat

The word 'habitat' (from the Latin word for 'it inhabits') is used to describe a type of ecosystem in which one or more particular organisms live.

Habitats can be found in many different forms across the world, both on land and in water.

Examples of terrestrial habitats include grassland (such as the South American pampas), heathland and moorland, including those found in the Scottish Highlands, as well as deciduous, coniferous and mixed woods. Aquatic habitats occur in ponds, lakes, streams, rivers, seas and oceans. In between, there are many others such as peat bogs (like those covering much of Siberia), marshland (for example, the Camargue in France), estuaries, dune systems and beaches.

Each of these has many, many variants, some of which are only found in specific climate zones. Without the niche features of the environments they evolved in, most species are unable to survive. Consequently, it is vital that the world's rich diversity of habitats is preserved, if more extinctions are to be avoided.

Unfortunately, habitat loss is now one of the greatest threats faced by the natural environment and, thanks to human activities, many of the world's most species-rich places are currently being destroyed at an unprecedented rate. This is especially true of tropical rainforests where vast areas of the jungle are being cut down. This is to make way for agriculture, industry or, increasingly, for residential purposes.

Heathlands

As far as habitats go, heathlands are often overlooked, since they are not seen as particularly glamorous places.

Heathlands occur in many parts of the world, and can be found more or less anywhere where there is a combination of soil that is free-draining (often sandy) and lacking in plant nutrients, both in warm or hot temperatures.

Heathlands are usually populated by low scrub growing on dry, acidic, fairly barren soils, often with ground-hugging herbage between larger plants such as heather and gorse.

The fauna and flora found in these habitats have adapted to life in often fairly inhospitable conditions and usually include a wide variety of insects such as grasshoppers, ants, butterflies and bees. These are then hunted by birds like flycatchers and shrikes, with finches eating the plant seeds. There are often also significant numbers of reptiles such as snakes and lizards.

In many developed countries, heathlands are usually the first places to be exploited for use as industrial sites or for residential housing. Consequently, many once common plants and animals have become rare or endangered. These fragile places therefore need to be preserved if the species that live in them stand any realistic chance of survival.

See: *Endangered Species*, page 75; *Insects*, page 114; *Reptiles*, page 160

Herbicides

Herbicides are chemicals that are specially formulated to kill plants.

Some herbicides – such as those based on glyphosate – are intended to destroy any vegetation they come into contact with, whereas others – such as those containing Mecoprop-P – only target certain kinds. These are known as non-selective and selective herbicides respectively.

Herbicides that take a long time to decompose into harmless chemicals are also seen as 'persistent forms'. Until relatively recently, large quantities of persistent toxins were used, and these contaminated both the soil and the ground water, causing all manner of environmental problems. A number of health concerns have also been raised regarding their effect on humans.

In 1971 the herbicide industry produced an organophosphate (based on esters of phosphoric acid) chemical known as glyphosate. Marketed under a variety of brand names, this non-selective substance has a very short decomposition time. If it is sprayed onto green vegetation, it is absorbed and kills the plant by interfering with its internal chemistry.

As these chemical reactions do not exist in animals, it is a relatively safe material. That being said, some of the formulations it is used in involve other substances that can be harmful to the environment.

In addition, a number of crops have been carefully bred to be resistant to glyphosate-based herbicides. This means that they can be sprayed and only the weeds around those crops, rather than the crops thesmelves, will be killed off.

Herbivores

Herbivores are a class of mammals that feed entirely on vegetative matter.

Herbivores are grouped into three orders – the Sirenia, which includes the marine-dwelling manatee, the Perissodactyla, which contains creatures like the horse, zebra and rhinoceros and the Artiodactyla. This last group is made up of such animals as deer, pigs, camels, giraffes, hippos and antelope.

The plants eaten by herbivores have such low nutritional values that enormous quantities are required for these large animals to be able to sustain themselves.

Such materials also contain large amounts of cellulose, which is very hard to break down. Herbivores have therefore evolved a variety of specialized digestive systems to deal with it. The predominant method is that of ruminants, whereby food is eaten and then later regurgitated in the form of cud. This is then chewed for a second time and swallowed again. Examples of ruminants include cattle, goats and sheep.

Some herbivores, such as rhinos, live most of their lives as individuals while others, including zebras and certain species of deer and antelope, mass together in large herds. They are found wherever there are sufficient quantities of plants, in places ranging from the Arctic tundras to the rainforest jungles.

Humidity

Humidity is a word used to describe the amount of water vapour that is present in a given volume of air.

Humidity is a very important factor in the environment. Many animals and plants can only survive if they receive sufficient atmospheric moisture. Especially sensitive are those creatures, such as frogs, toads and newts, which are highly dependent on water. Many of these will die quickly if their skins dry out, and so they are only found in places with damp air.

There are three main types of humidity – relative, specific and absolute. The most common is relative humidity. This is widely used in meteorology, and is expressed as the ratio of the amount of water vapour in the air to the amount that it is possible for it to hold. When the air is fully saturated – that is, not able to hold any more moisture – the relative humidity figure is 100 per cent.

The actual amount of this to reach saturation point varies significantly with temperature. At 25°C (77°F) for instance, a cubic metre of air can hold 23g/0.8oz of water, but at 32°F (0°C) this drops to 5g/0.1oz.

In several parts of the world activities such as deforestation have caused local climate changes. These have led to significant humidity variations, and many organisms have become endangered or even extinct as a direct result.

Hurricanes

Hurricanes are severe tropical storms that can cause significant damage to the natural environment as well as to human lives and property.

Referred to as 'cyclones' in the Indian and South Pacific Oceans and 'typhoons' in the Western North Pacific and Philippines, hurricanes start out as swirling depressions that gradually grow in intensity until they are strong enough to be classified as storms. These usually abate before long, but if the conditions are right they will continue to increase in strength if there is sufficient vertical wind shear.

A storm is considered to have become a hurricane when its average wind speeds rise above 119kph/74mph. On average there are about 100 hurricanes a year, with most of these occurring in the Indian Ocean as the result of a meteorological region known as the Inter Tropical Convergence Zone. This is an area where there are lots of thunderstorms. When these are combined with warm seas, hurricanes often form.

One of the main types of environmental damage they cause is erosion, which often occurs as the result of the severe flooding that occurs after a storm surge. Sand dunes – which are important but fragile habitats – can be completely washed away, endangering many species of plants and animals. The strong winds also often uproot large trees, again, damaging precious ecosystems.

Over the last 100 years there have been over 20 hurricanes that have each caused more than $1 billion damage.

See: *Cyclone*, page 62; *Thunderstorms*, page 184

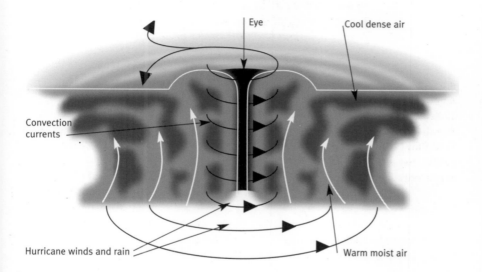

Eye

Cool dense air

Convection currents

Hurricane winds and rain

Warm moist air

The formation of a hurricane.

Hydroelectric Power

Hydroelectric power is obtained by using the potential energy of falling water to turn a turbine that is linked to an electrical generator.

In its simplest form, hydroelectric power results from a stream that is ducted over a chute and onto a paddle wheel. **More complex systems involve axial flow turbines or elegant arrays of booms that are operated by the movement of the tides.**

Although such systems are very cheap to run, substantial investment is usually needed to pay for their installation. They produce very little, if any, pollution once commissioned, although any environmental calculations must take into account the implication of their manufacturing and transportation to site.

Many hydroelectric systems are powered by water that is stored in reservoirs. While the electricity generation part of the equation may be environmentally friendly, these man-made features can be the exact opposite.

Not only are large areas of often ecologically important habitats flooded to build them, but in tropical regions they often produce more pollution than if the electricity had been obtained using conventional fossil fuels. This is because the vegetation that grows up around them is regularly flooded – it then dies and rots, releasing large amounts of greenhouse gases.

Hydrogen Fuel

Hydrogen is the lightest of all the elements, and is a particularly flammable gas. It can be converted to provide heat, light and power.

When burned in air, hydrogen combines with oxygen to form water vapour. An excellent fuel, it does not produce the harmful pollutants released by fossil-derived equivalents.

Hydrogen is very difficult to store; it needs to be kept in high-pressure vessels that are both heavy and bulky.

Hydrogen can be produced in a number of ways. It can be made from such products as coal gas, natural gas, Liquid Petroleum Gas, and from biomass, as well as by the electrolysis of sea water and microbial fermentation.

Hydrogen can be used to power internal combustion engines in the same way as those fuelled by gasoline, or it can power fuel cells. These use combustion of hydrogen to generate electricity – this is then used to power electric motors in a pollutant-free manner.

Although its combustion is inherently environmentally friendly, it is not without its problems as a fuel. It is almost impossible to manufacture and store hydrogen without small amounts escaping into the atmosphere. If it became a widely used source of energy, some experts fear that it could build up in the higher levels of the atmosphere, causing problems in the ozone layer.

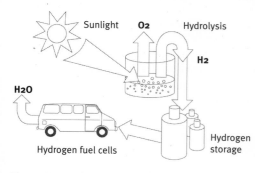

The production of hydrogen fuel.

Hydrologic Cycle

The name 'hydrologic cycle' is given to the way in which water journeys from the atmosphere onto the Earth's surface and back into the air again.

The hydrologic cycle begins when water – either from damp ground or a body of water – evaporates from its liquid state into vapour. Since this is warm and light, it rises up into the sky.

As the vapour rises it begins to cool down, condensing into droplets which accumulate in vast numbers, forming clouds. These will freeze into minute crystals if the temperature is low enough. If they grow to a size where they become too heavy to remain in suspension, they begin to fall towards the ground as precipitation.

Depending on the prevailing atmospheric conditions, this precipitation can take any one of several forms. For example, if the temperature is cold enough, it will fall as snow, sleet or hail. If not, it descends as rain.

Over the last 50 years, humankind has made repeated attempts to control the factors that determine when rain will fall. So far, these have been unsuccessful but, as technology moves forward, it may one day become a viable proposition.

In many parts of the world access to fresh water is extremely limited, and it is thought that local and regional arguments over supplies could even trigger major wars.

Indicator Species

The term 'indicator species' describes an organism that can be used to gauge the health of a particular ecosystem.

The various species chosen to test the health of an ecosystem are typically very sensitive to environmental changes, and so if their populations change suddenly, it can provide an early warning that something is wrong.

The cause of fluctuation may be due to an event such as a chemical spill or some other source of pollution, or it could be the result of other human activities. Alternatively, it may be down to more natural occurrences such as climate change, volcanic eruptions or an increase in predator numbers.

Indicator species can also be selected to mark the edges of a specific ecosystem. For instance, certain plants are regularly used for this purpose in many parts of the world, including the Chihuahua Desert, which covers parts of northern Mexico and the southwestern United States, as well as several of the world's cloud forests.

Lichens are an excellent example of indicator species, as they are very sensitive to air pollutants, especially sulphur dioxide, which is a substance emitted by industrial processes and volcanoes. Other examples of indicator species include the Atlantic Puffin, which is sensitive to over-fishing, and various amphibians which cannot tolerate water pollution.

Insects

Insects are small invertebrates that can be found in almost all the terrestrial habitats on Earth, with the exception of central Antarctica.

Insects vary tremendously in form and lifestyle, although they share a few basic characteristics.

These include a metamorphic life history, whereby they go through a number of stages, and the adults all have bodies that are divided into three parts, namely the head, thorax and abdomen.

The head carries the eyes, antennae and mouth parts as well as the brain. The thorax is attached to the wings and legs, and also houses the flight muscles. The abdomen contains the respiratory, reproductive and digestive organs.

Insects do not have an internal bone structure. Instead, they have a hard external shell called an exoskeleton which is made of chitin. This acts as both a protective shield and a platform for all the appendages and muscles.

A typical insect begins life as an egg which hatches into a larva, and after growing to a certain size it metamorphoses into a pupa and finally into an adult.

There are currently more than one million insects known to science, but the actual figure may be at least 10 times higher than this.

Jet Streams

Jet streams are high-altitude, rapidly moving rivers of air.

Jet streams are usually quite narrow in relation to their length. They are usually found between 10–12km/6–12mi above the Earth's surface in an atmospheric layer known as the tropopause, which lies between the troposphere and the stratosphere.

Jet streams form in a number of different areas, including the tropics, and one is usually found in each polar region. The high-latitude streams arise in the Westerlies zone when low-level warm air moves northwards and meets southward-flowing cold air. This forces it to rise, and as it does so it speeds up.

They can reach speeds of 547kph/340mph, although the figure varies with the time of year. In the winter, the temperature difference between the polar region and the tropics is greatest, and this condition generates the highest speeds. Conversely, there is less difference in temperatures during the summer, and therefore the jet streams move more slowly as a result.

There is so much energy in the jet streams that if only one per cent were harnessed, it could supply all the world's energy needs. This is such an attractive idea that many institutions are studying ways in which this could be made possible. Proposed methods range from self-powered helicopters and giant kites to helium balloons, all of which carry on-board generators and are tethered to the ground with electrical cables.

Köppen Climate Classification System

The Köppen Climate Classification System is used to categorize the climates of particular places.

Based on the overall patterns of weather over many years, the Köppen Climate Classification System takes into account the characteristic seasonal weather fluctuations, as well as less frequent events such as droughts and hurricanes.

The system was devised in 1900, by Wladimir Köppen, a Russian–German climatologist. It separates the global climates into five categories. These are denoted A–E in the chart below, with a further four sub-groups which are labelled f–w.

THE KOPPEN CLIMATE CLASSIFICATION SYSTEM	
A	This denotes moist tropical climates with high temperatures and large amounts of rainfall.
B	This denotes dry climates with low rainfall and a wide variation in daily temperatures. The category is further divided into subgroups labelled 'S' for semi-arid or steppe environments, and 'W' for arid or desert environments.
C	This denotes places with warm, dry summers and cold, wet winters. Typically, these environments are found in mid-latitudes.
D	This denotes the climates found in the interiors of large continental masses, where rainfall is moderate and temperatures vary widely during the seasons.
E	This denotes polar climates where permanent ice and tundra can be found, and temperatures rise above freezing for only about four months of the year.

The table below lists the sub-groupings f–w, each designated by a lowercase letter. There are other, more detailed sub-categories that go on to specify maximum and minimum temperatures.

f	Areas where there is no dry season, and similar levels of precipitation throughout the year.
m	Areas where there is a rainforest climate with a short dry season.
m	Areas where there is a dry season in the summer.
w	Areas where there is a dry season in the winter.

See: *Drought*, page 69; *Hurricanes*, page 108–109

Kyoto Protocol

The Kyoto Protocol is an international agreement that was devised with the intention of cutting the amount of greenhouse gas emissions.

After two-and-a-half years of intense negotiation, the protocol was adopted on 11 December 1997 at the Kyoto conference in Japan but it did not come into force until after it was ratified on 16 February 2005.

In 2012, the protocol will expire, but discussions are underway to construct a succession agreement. Although it has received a lot of publicity, it is, in fact, only one part of a much larger structure known as the UN Framework Convention on Climate Change (UNFCCC), by which conferences are held to share information on greenhouse-gas emissions, as well as discuss national policies and set out best practice.

It also seeks to identify the possible impact of climate change and makes recommendations for the best strategies for dealing with any such changes. The Convention was adopted in 1992 and has since been ratified by 172 countries. Some of these have been given specific targets for reductions in their emissions levels, but the vast majority have no obligations other than monitoring and recording their outputs. Australia, Kazakhstan and the United States are the only countries that have not signed up to the Convention yet.

The Kyoto Protocol was set up in such a way that countries which exceed their specified levels can offset their excess contributions through a process known as 'emissions trading'. This is where countries that produce less than their specified amounts of atmospheric pollutants can sell their unused quotas to other governments or companies.

Lightning

Lightning is generated by the accumulation of differing electrical charges in the clouds that make up a thunderstorm system.

When positive and negative charges in a series of clouds have built up to the point where they can no longer be sustained, they either discharge to a neighbouring cloud or to the ground. This occurs in the form of a powerful electrical spark called lightning.

The amount of energy within such a strike is enormous, and it heats the air it travels through to around 27,760°C (50,000°F). Such a high temperature cannot be maintained for more than a few milliseconds and after the strike has passed the air quickly cools again.

A by-product of this superheating and cooling is an incredibly loud acoustic shock wave that we refer to as 'thunder'. Each strike is typically between 2 and 10 miles long and carries about 100 million volts with a current of around 10,000 amps.

At any given time, there are many thunderstorms occurring around the world, and these create between 50 and 100 lightning strikes every second of every day. Ironically, despite these very regular occurrences, lightning is still one of the most poorly understood aspects of meteorology.

Light Pollution

Light pollution is a modern-day issue that, perhaps surprisingly, receives little attention.

Despite its low profile, light pollution can cause a number of problems for the environment.

At its simplest, it means that city-dwelling humans are unable to see the stars properly. This is because all the artificial light produced by street lights and illuminated signs, for example, reflects off particles in the atmosphere, creating a glow that is many times brighter than the light from the night sky.

Most of this light is lost and, thus, is responsible for the unnecessary consumption of large amounts of energy. This, in turn, produces atmospheric pollutants and wastes valuable resources.

Light pollution damages ecosystems in other ways, too. It can, for instance, interfere with the lives of insects, which are either attracted to it or are unable to find mates because of disorientation.

Fireflies, for example, use light to signal to one another, and the presence of such objects as domestic lamps and streetlights can significantly alter their behaviour patterns.

Plants can have their metabolic processes disrupted as well, since they often use daylight length to determine when to produce flowers and so on. In a similar manner, human sleep patterns can be altered by exposure to strong lights.

Littoral Zone

'Littoral zone' describes the area that is regularly swept by the tides. As a result, high and low water marks can be clearly seen.

For the organisms that live there, the littoral zone is one of the most challenging of the world's environments as conditions change markedly, depending on the state of the tide.

There are many different kinds of littoral ecosystems, such as rocky seashores where large outcrops of rock are interspersed with rock pools. These are often home to a spectacular array of different life forms, each honed by evolution to fit a particular environmental niche.

A good example is that of the limpet, a marine gastropod that has developed an armour-plated shell and an incredibly strong muscular foot. This enables it to live in places where powerful waves break regularly.

Other shorelines may be composed of sand or mud, and these are home to an entirely different group of organisms, where burrowing is the predominant lifestyle.

The shifting nature of the substrates means that littoral zones are usually home to only a very few species of seaweeds. Despite this, they are considered to be rich and diverse places.

Splash Zone	High Water Spring
Littoral (Intertidal)	High Tide
	Low Tide
	Low Water Spring
Sub Littoral	
Lower Sub Littoral	

Mammals

Mammals are a group of warm-blooded vertebrates that include creatures as diverse as humans, apes, cats, dogs, cows, sheep and whales.

There are about 5,000 different species categorized into about 26 different orders.

As well as warm blood and backbones or vertebrae, mammals also share three defining characteristics that set them apart from all other animals. Mammals have three middle ear bones in each ear; they also suckle their offspring with milk produced from mammary glands on the ventral side of the body. Finally, they have hair on their bodies.

The hair is composed of a protein called keratin and serves both as a thermal insulator and to provide coloration. Often this hair is in the form of a pattern. That displayed by zebras, for example, serves as a form of camouflage, breaking up their outline and helping shield them from potential predators.

Other mammmals use colour in different ways. For skunks it is a form of visible warning, while mandrills use it to convey messages about breeding status. The hair of some mammals, such as hedgehogs and porcupines, has evolved into sharp quills which act as an effective defence mechanism against would-be predators.

The 5,000 or so mammal species are split into three sub-divisions: the monotremes (egg-laying mammals such as spiny anteaters and duck-billed platypus); the marsupials (those with pouches for their young); and the placental mammals (those which nourish their unborn young with placentas).

Marsupials

Marsupials are distinguished from other mammals by the presence of a pouch in the females, used to help rear their young.

Typical examples of common marsupials include kangaroos, Koalas and possums. Others are much more rare, and include the Duck-billed Platypus, the Quoll and the numbat. Some, such as the Thylacine or Tasmanian Tiger (marsupial wolf), have recently become extinct, due to humankind's activities.

The vast majority of marsupials are only found in Australasia, although there are a few that live elsewhere. The Common Opossum, found across most of the Americas, is the best example of this.

Marsupials evolved at a time when the landmass that later became Australia was isolated from the places where other mammals were living. As a consequence, these animals have many unique physical features and highly unusual life histories in comparison to other mammals.

When humankind first populated the areas inhabited by marsupials some 30,000 years ago, there were far more species than remain today. Tragically, many of these were hunted to extinction or succumbed to the introduction of alien species such as dogs and rats.

When Europeans settled there in the 1700s, many more became extinct as the result of habitat loss, over-hunting and the introduction of further alien species.

Mediterranean (Chaparral) Climate

Mediterranean, or 'chaparral', climates are very hot and dry in the summer but relatively mild and moist in the winter.

In Mediterranean or chaparral climates frosts are uncommon and temperatures rarely dip below freezing point. Springtime is often marked by enormous swathes of vividly coloured flowers that exploit the brief chance to bloom before the onset of the summer's heat.

Peak temperatures tend to be in the region of 40°C (104°F) and this, coupled with very low precipitation, gives rise to very arid conditions. As a result, only certain forms of flora can survive. These include grasses that can cope with prolonged desiccation, as well as vegetation such as cork oaks, pine, olive and eucalyptus trees.

Wildfires are common in these areas. Some are started naturally – lightning strikes are a particularly common cause. Many are deliberately set by misguided people, however, and this not only presents a serious threat to life and property, but also causes terrible environmental problems.

Examples of areas with Mediterranean climates are found in central and southern California, parts of coastal western, eastern and southern Australia, the Chilean coast, South Africa and, of course, much of the Mediterranean region.

Mesosphere

The Mesosphere is a layer in the middle atmosphere that lies above the stratosphere and below the thermosphere.

Beginning at a height of about 50km/35 mi, the mesosphere rises to an elevation of around 85km/53mi above the Earth's surface.

The mesosphere is the coldest part of the entire atmosphere, with temperatures falling (as altitude increases) to around -98°C (-145°F) in its upper reaches.

Although the air in the mesosphere has a very low density, there are still enough molecules to generate considerable friction for any meteorites that enter it. As a result, almost all of the millions that do so every day burn up well before they reach the surface.

The mesosphere is the least studied part of the atmosphere, being above the altitude capabilities of fixed-wing aircraft, but below those for spacecraft. Since it is a vital component in the way that sunlight heats our atmosphere, the *Atlas–1* Spacelab mission series was launched in 1992 to examine it more closely.

In particular, the scientific instruments it carried recorded data on the ways in which the mesosphere interacts with the thermosphere and the magnetosphere. This contributed significant amounts of new information on the subject and has helped meteorologists to understand more about global warming.

Methane Fuel

Methane is the chemical name for what is commonly referred to as natural or marsh gas.

Methane is a valuable fuel that is mostly obtained from reserves that reside deep underground. These are the by-product of the decay of organic material that was laid down many millions of years ago and then buried over geologic time.

It is also produced by refuse and landfill sites, as well as from the decay of agricultural waste and the output from sewage farms. While methane can be used to power vehicles, it is more often used to generate electricity for domestic cooking or to heat water.

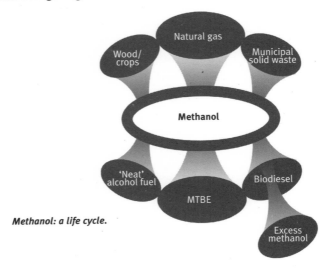

Methanol: a life cycle.

Giving rise to less carbon dioxide and other atmospheric pollutants than equivalent fossil fuels, methane can also be produced by synthetic means via electrolysis or by extraction from coal.

The most promising route from an environmental perspective is by the fermentation of industrial agricultural waste. This not only provides a viable alternative to fossil fuels, but also prevents large amounts of methane from reaching the atmosphere. As a greenhouse gas, it is about 25 times more harmful than carbon dioxide.

Methane is not without its problems as an alternative source of fuel for vehicles though. Since it is a gas, it needs to be kept in suitably pressurized storage vessels, and is therefore more difficult to distribute than liquid equivalents.

See: *Fossil Fuels*, pages 86–87; *Greenhouse Effect*, page 99

Methane Pollution

From an environmental perspective methane (or marsh gas) has both good and bad properties.

While it provides an excellent alternative to fossil fuels, methane is an extremely harmful greenhouse gas, being around 25 times more destructive than carbon dioxide. It is, however, less persistent, as it decomposes within about a decade, compared to carbon dioxide, which lasts over 100 years.

Methane is released into the air by both natural and artificial processes. It is produced by the decomposition of organic matter, as well as by living plants and animals. The amount of methane in the atmosphere has risen by about 150 per cent since the start of the Industrial Revolution in the mid 18th century.

Currently, its concentration at the surface averages out at about 1,750 parts per billion. Interestingly, this figure was 1,000 times higher early in the formation of the Earth's atmosphere.

As photosynthetic plants evolved though, oxygen became a major constituent, and this vastly increased the rate at which methane breaks down. Consequently, its levels began to fall dramatically, and eventually they stabilized at concentrations similar to those of today.

There are concerns that the vast amounts of methane gas trapped beneath the ice in the permafrost regions of the Arctic might be released into the atmosphere as a result of global warming.

Molluscs

*The best-known molluscs are slugs,
snails and seashells.*

Molluscs are a very diverse group of creatures that include bivalves, tusk shells, chitons, octopus, squid and cuttlefish.

Molluscs vary in size from tiny snails measuring just a few millimetres long to the Colossal Squid (*Mesonychoteuthis hamiltoni*), which, it is believed, can grow up to as much as a gigantic 14m/46ft long.

Slugs are well known as ubiquitous pests to gardeners the world over and, although they lack shells, they are, in fact, members of the snail family.

There are about 112,000 different species of mollusc, with the vast majority being marine dwellers. They can be broadly split into two categories: predators and those that feed on vegetative matter.

The plant feeders tend to be slow-moving and have heavily armoured shells; examples include chitons and limpets. The predatory molluscs include fast-moving hunters such as the squid, octopus and cuttlefish, which feed on anything they can catch, from fish to crustaceans. Others, such as the deadly textile cones, move much more slowly, but with equally lethal results.

Molluscs are important components of the planet's environment. They consume vast amounts of dead animal and plant material, recycling it back into the ecosystem in the form of vital nutrients.

Native vs Introduced Species

A native species is an organism that occurs naturally in a particular region and is often referred to as being indigenous.

There are many examples of native species of flora, fauna and micro-organisms occurring all over the world. These include the oak tree in the United Kingdom, the kiwi in New Zealand, the eucalyptus tree in Australia and the impala (African antelope) in Africa.

However, native species do not include those which have been introduced – either deliberately or accidentally by humankind.

According to the *Audit of Non-native Species in England* (2005), there are c. 2,721 non-native species and hybrids present in England, although this drops to just 1,413 species once garden animals, fungi and rare vascular plants are taken out of the equation. The report concludes that most are beneficial to humans, constituting many of our crops and domestic animals.

The rabbit has been common in the British Isles for about 5,000 years. It was originally introduced by the Romans as a source of food. Similarly, horses are not native to North America, but were introduced about 400 years ago by European settlers. Neither of these introductions caused any significant displacements of similar animals, but that is not always the case.

In the 19th century, the North American Grey Squirrel, which had originally been introduced to the United Kingdom as an ornamental species, soon replaced the native Red Squirrel.

There are many other instances in which the effects of introductions have been even more serious. An example of this occurred after the Cane Toad was introduced into Australia in 1935. Originally intended to help combat sugar cane pests, the toad, whose skin is highly toxic, quickly became a serious problem when it became apparent that it fed on many native animals as well as pests.

Natural Disasters

Natural disasters include such events as volcanic eruptions, earthquakes and tsunamis.

Natural disasters can have a variety of serious consequences for both the environment and humans living in the region. In some cases, they can cause local, or even widespread, extinctions.

Such disasters can vary from very restricted occurrences, such as avalanches, to asteroid strikes and other potentially global catastrophes.

Some experts believe that the Cretaceous–Triassic extinction event (about 65.5 million years ago) was caused by an asteroid hitting the Earth, throwing up so much debris that the Sun was blocked out to such an extent that most organisms were not able to survive.

Volcanoes can also cause problems on a global scale, both by blocking out sunlight as well as by releasing vast quantities of toxic materials, such as sulphur dioxide, into the atmosphere. Tsunamis are powerful waves, triggered by impulses such as submarine landslides and earthquakes. They can cause enormous amounts of damage to coastal regions.

Those species that are restricted to supra-littoral zones are very vulnerable to such events, particularly those which have come under significant pressure as a result of human activities.

Although some natural disasters do not have as severe an effect as volcanoes, they can still have far-reaching environmental consequences. A single hurricane, for example, can uproot and blow large trees across thousands of square miles. This can displace large numbers of organisms that depend on the trees and, in some cases result in their own extinction.

See: *Littoral Zone*, page 121; *Tsunami*, page 191; *Volcanoes*, page 194

Nature Reserves

Nature reserves are areas that have been specifically set aside by governments, institutions or individuals as places in which wildlife is encouraged to flourish, or special features of some kind are preserved.

Nature reserves are found in every part of the world. Examples of human-made nature reserves include those featuring ancient structures, such as the stone circles found in England at Stonehenge and the White Peak District of Derbyshire, as well as monuments, cave paintings and sculptures. Particularly important waterfalls, canyons, hill ranges or islands fall into the category of natural nature reserves.

Nature reserves can occur on land or in the sea, and access to them is sometimes restricted. Most have to be carefully managed and so require significant resources to fund the required human power and equipment.

In some areas, this may consist of the prevention and control of wildfires, whereas in others anti-poaching may be necessary.

Most of the world's nature reserves have to be closely monitored to ensure that no animals or plants are liable to become overpopulated. Unfortunately, if this happens, it upsets the balance of the ecosystem and the more sensitive species may not survive.

Overpopulation can be a problem if there are no natural predators, in which case species like herbivores, for example, may cause irreversible damage to the habitat. Therefore, some sort of artificial control is required.

Nematode

*Nematodes, also known as roundworms,
are multicellular animals.*

Found in almost every environment on Earth, about three-quarters of the 20,000 or so species of nematodes are parasites living off other animals or within the tissues of plants.

Although they are unable to fly, they can be found in most of the creatures that do. A large number of nematodes live in the soil, where they either prey on different types of invertebrates or feed on vegetable matter. Some are even found in the most extreme and inhospitable climates in the world, such as the frozen wastes of Central Antarctica, where the only other life forms are microbes and microscopic algae.

As a group of animals, nematodes are increasingly being used in support of environmentally friendly methods of horticulture and agriculture. This is because certain species are particularly adept at controlling the numbers of some of the most significant commercial pests. The main benefits are that they are relatively cheap to use and can also be very effective.

Consequently, far fewer insecticides are being used, which not only saves money but also helps reduce the quantity of toxic chemicals that are released into the environment.

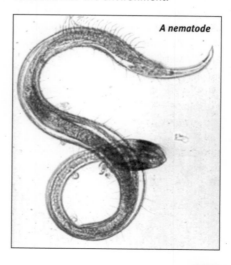

A nematode

Nitrates

Nitrates are chemical compounds that are formed when nitric acid reacts with an appropriate substance to form a nitrate salt.

From an environmental perspective nitrates are essential building blocks for life. Despite this, they are also major ecosystem pollutants.

One of the main sources of nitrate contamination is from agriculture. The widespread and indiscriminate use of nitrate fertilizers results in these chemicals being washed into waterways, and from there into the sea. This causes all manner of problems as many aquatic animals cannot tolerate raised levels and die if exposed to them.

Conversely, many species of algae thrive in increased nitrate levels and can reproduce so quickly that they starve the water of sunlight and oxygen. This can have catastrophic effects on all of the other organisms in their proximity.

Nitrates are also present in large quantities in human sewage and farmyard slurries. If allowed to enter waterways, their presence can result in the deaths of large numbers of animals and plants.

At sea, increased nitrate levels have been linked to the bleaching of coral reefs. This is where the increased nutrient levels have interfered with the internal chemistry of the algae that live inside the coral polyps. Since the corals depend on these for their survival, they soon die off. This is thought to have been responsible for significant amounts of damage to coral reefs in recent years.

See: *Coral Reefs*, page 57; *Environment*, page 77

Nitric Oxides

Major chemical contaminants of the atmosphere, nitric oxides are produced by a number of different processes, some natural, and some man-made.

The processes that create nitric oxides include lightning, exhaust fumes and many industrial activities.

There are several different nitrogen compounds that fall within this category, and they are often referred to as 'NOx', where 'N' is the chemical symbol for nitrogen, 'O' is that of oxygen, and 'x' stands for the number of oxygen atoms.

Nitrous oxide, for instance, has the formula N_2O. It is a highly reactive substance that is commonly called laughing gas and was, until relatively recently, widely used as an anaesthetic. In the presence of sunlight, nitrous oxide quickly reacts with other atmospheric components, forming various other nitric oxides or acids.

These include NO_2, which is nitrogen dioxide, or HNO_3 (nitric acid).

Ultimately, most atmospheric nitric oxides end up polluting the Earth in the form of acid rain. This can cause serious consequences for many animals and plants, with sensitive species unable to survive if subjected to prolonged periods of exposure.

In some regions of Scandinavia, for instance, vast areas of pine trees were killed as the direct result of acid rain which arose from gases released by Eastern European industrial facilities. Fortunately, once nitric oxides have penetrated the ground, they are usually broken down relatively quickly and used as a source of nitrogen by various soil microbes and plants.

Noise Pollution

Noise pollution is an often overlooked aspect of environmental damage.

The problems caused by noise pollution are now becoming better understood; regulations concerning its abatement are slowly being put into force in many countries.

The two main forms of noise pollution occur either in open air or underwater. The former is usually caused by such activities as aircraft, railways and road transport, as well as industrial machinery and domestic or leisure activities. The latter is typically generated by ships' engines and propellers, sonar detection systems and the machinery used by the oil industry.

While noise pollution can be extremely stressful and annoying for humans, it can significantly disrupt the lives of many kinds of animals. Certain birds, for instance, may be unable to use what would otherwise be suitable breeding sites, and many animals which rely on acoustic signals for mate attraction may suffer from markedly reduced reproductive success in noisy areas.

Such pressures may push some endangered species towards extinction. Many marine animals, especially whales, dolphins and porpoises, have suffered very badly in recent years as a direct consequence of the use of high-strength naval sonar systems. These appear to cause serious disorientation and, tragically, have resulted in many of these creatures being beached and killed.

Nuclear Power

Nuclear power is a form of energy that is obtained by controlled nuclear fission.

Nuclear fission is a complicated chain reaction which runs at the sub-atomic scale, releasing enormous quantities of energy in the form of heat. This is then used to convert water into steam, which is in turn employed to drive a steam turbine that is most commonly connected to an electricity generator.

Although nuclear power stations produce very little in the way of pollutants in normal use, they are not popular with many environmentalists. This is because they create highly toxic radioactive wastes as by-products that persist for many thousands of years.

Consequently, it is very hard to find safe ways of disposing of them.

A further issue is that of operating accidents. The most famous example occurred in the Ukraine (part of the former Soviet Union) in 1986 and involved the Chernobyl reactor. Following an equipment malfunction the core melted down, releasing large quantities of radioactive poisons straight into the atmosphere.

In spite of these dangers, though, many environmental experts say that nuclear power offers the only realistic and clean way of providing humankind's energy requirements for the foreseeable future.

See: *Radioactive Waste*, page 155

Oceans

Oceans, which are large bodies of salt water, cover nearly three-quarters of the planet and contain more than 97 per cent of all the world's water.

There are five main oceans – the Atlantic, Pacific, Indian, Arctic and Southern Oceans – which are, in fact, all seamlessly interconnected despite artificially imposed boundaries.

The world's oceans provide an incredible amount of habitat for living organisms. Indeed, around 99 per cent of all the space occupied by inhabited ecosystems on Earth is found in the oceans.

Although the oceans have an average depth of just under 4km/2.5mi, there are many abysses which are considerably deeper. The Mariana Trench in the western Pacific – the deepest of these – measures 11,033m/36,198ft, in what is known as the Challenger Deep.

At such depths, the pressure is almost unimaginably high and nearly 1,100 times greater than is found in the atmosphere at sea level. Consequently, any life forms that are found in the lower parts of the oceans must be very highly specialized to survive the constraints of such habitats. To this day, experts believe many remain unknown to science and there are undoubtedly some wonderful discoveries yet to be made.

Omnivores

Omnivores are organisms that eat both plant and animal matter. Humankind is predominantly made up of omnivores.

Many omnivores do not have fixed diets, but exploit whatever opportunities they can find. This is especially true in areas in which there are marked seasonal changes and the type of food that is available varies significantly as the year passes.

The diversity of foodstuffs consumed is reflected in the fact that few omnivores have specialized digestive tracts. This means that they are unable to eat low-energy substances like grasses, as these contain a great deal of cellulose. In their place, higher energy materials – including fruit, eggs, meat and fish, for instance – are chosen. Many omnivores are proficient hunters, too. Examples of these include mammals such as humans, chimpanzees, squirrels and mice, as well as birds like crows, magpies and jays. Others are primarily scavengers on dead animals.

There are omnivorous insects, too. Many wasps, for instance, can often be seen feeding on items such as rotting fruit, as well as on other insects.

A large number of omnivores have adapted to living around human settlements, feeding on the large amounts of refuse that are allowed to accumulate there. Examples of these include rats, seagulls, racoons and opossums.

Organic Farming

Organic farming differs from conventional farming in avoiding the use of synthetic chemicals like growth-promotion agents, fertilizers, herbicides and pesticides, as well as genetically modified organisms.

In organic farming, natural alternatives are employed wherever possible, but under certain circumstances the use of some synthetic substances is permitted. The preferred agents include nematode parasites, for example, which are used to control insect pests and animal manure as a replacement for chemical fertilizers.

There are also a number of management techniques that can be taken to improve the quality and quantity of harvested produce. Crop rotation regimes, for instance, reduce the spread of agricultural diseases, and mechanical weeding can remove the need for herbicides. In many countries, farmers are only allowed to label their produce as 'organic' if they adhere to certain strict regulations. This involves official inspections and certification, as well as adherence to certain policies, such as promoting biodiversity, ensuring the well-being of livestock and protecting the land. All these measures add significantly to the overall cost, however, and this is reflected in increased consumer prices. In spite of this, the market has grown considerably in recent years, and is expected to continue doing so for the foreseeable future.

See: *Nematode,* page 133; *Pesticides,* page 147

Organism

*The term 'organism' is applied to any living entity,
be it a plant, animal or a fungus.*

The simplest examples of organisms only have one cell and can vary in size from the smallest bacteria, at around one micron across, to certain protozoans which may be over 500 microns in diameter.

These are often referred to as micro-organisms, single-celled organisms or unicellular organisms.

Complex organisms, on the other hand, may have many millions of cells and include everything from tiny nematode worms and algae to mammals, such as humans and elephants, as well as flowering plants and trees.

Organisms can be found in most places on Earth – from the frozen wastes of the Antarctic interior to the skies high above our heads. They all need air, water and food in order to survive, as well as an environment that meets their specific physiological requirements. Usually, this involves certain temperature and humidity levels plus sufficient exposure to sunlight.

The places where they live are called habitats and the various organisms in a place together combine to form the living component of the local ecosystem.

Estimates of the total number of different organisms vary, as most of the smaller ones have yet to be identified.

Overpopulation

*The expression 'overpopulation' is used
when an organism's numbers exceed the
optimal level for its local environment, taking
into account the available resources.*

There are various interpretations of exactly what the definition of overpopulation really means. In the simplest terms, it may be just an arithmetic calculation concerning whether sufficient food and water are available.

In the wider context of the environment, however, any such study needs to consider the long-term effect of the population concerned on the ecosystems affected by it. If one takes the obvious example of humans, a given area may be able to sustain in good health a certain number of people, and so in the strictest sense, it is not overpopulated. These humans may, however, kill most of the animals in the area for food, cut down all the trees for fuel and generate significant amounts of pollution and waste.

Consequently, the local environment is badly damaged, and the community is unsustainable in the long term. In this case, it is certainly overpopulated. Sadly, with few exceptions, this is the case almost wherever mankind settles.

Other creatures go through regular cycles of population explosions and crashes. Many rodents, such as certain species of rats, mice and lemmings, may be rare in one season, but within two or three years reach such population densities that they form enormous swarms, which then leave the area seeking out new places to live.

Ozone Layer

Ozone is a colourless gas that is a relatively reactive and unstable form of oxygen and occurs in small quantities in the atmosphere.

Around 90 per cent of ozone gas is found at high altitudes in a region known as the ozone layer. This lies within the stratosphere and is responsible for filtering out most of the harmful components of the Sun's radiation, particularly ultraviolet rays.

Mesosphere (5–85km)

Stratosphere and natural protective ozone layer (17–50km)

Troposphere and tropospheric ozone (0–9/17km)

Altitude of most clouds

Somewhat paradoxically, although this feature makes life on Earth possible, ozone is, in fact, toxic when it occurs at low levels. It is also extremely sensitive to contact with certain atmospheric pollutants, especially chlorofluorocarbons (CFCs), which used to be commonly used in aerosols and refrigerators.

When this happens, the ozone breaks down and any ultraviolet protection it afforded the Earth is lost. In the 1970s, experts discovered that the ozone layer was becoming thinner due to such contamination and holes were appearing at both poles. A series of very strict regulations was subsequently passed to limit the use of CFCs and other similar harmful chemicals.

Most developed countries adhere to these regulations; some lack the resources to enforce the laws effectively and thus ozone-damaging chemicals are still released in some places.

Packaging

Almost every item that is sold in the modern world is contained in some form of packaging. While this can help protect the product inside, it is mostly there to entice the consumer.

A large proportion of packing materials are made from plastics and other substances that do not biodegrade. They are therefore harmful to the environment if not disposed of properly, but the problem, however, is exactly how to do this.

Landfill dumping is undesirable, as it destroys natural habitats and releases toxic chemicals. Incineration is also unacceptable, as it creates significant amounts of atmospheric pollution. Since most packaging is completely unnecessary, the simplest solution is just to do without it.

Where this is not practical, it can be re-designed using environmentally friendly materials – either with ones that biodegrade quickly or by using those which recycle well.

The best answer to this problem is to make packaging in such a way that it can be reused without having to undergo any kind of processing. There is widespread consumer support for this, and in many countries such philosophies are being reinforced by the imposition of tighter regulations.

Although such efforts are to be applauded, some governments penalize consumers by forcing them to pay higher taxes for the disposal of waste that is largely composed of excess packaging. This has the unfortunate consequence of encouraging the illegal dumping of domestic waste in environmentally sensitive areas.

Peat Bog

Peat is a natural material that is made up of dead plant matter.

In most cases, peat is composed of various kinds of mosses – especially sphagnum species – and lichens. Where it accumulates in places with poor drainage, it can quickly become waterlogged and form bogs. These are variously known around the world as moors, swamps, muskegs and mires.

In some regions, peat bogs cover vast areas – around three per cent of the world's land area is made up of peat wetlands. Many animals and plants have evolved to inhabit them and most cannot survive anywhere else. Bogs are therefore a very important part of the environment.

Peat is, however, a valuable commercial commodity, as it can be used both for fuel and for horticultural purposes. For this reason, many bogs have been drained and the peat removed. Over the last 20 years, the rate of bog destruction rose to such a level that several environmental organizations started campaigning to stop the trade in peat before it was too late.

Many peat substitutes are available for use in the garden and this has greatly reduced the pressure. Bog habitats are seen as conservation priorities around the world, and many agencies are doing their best to preserve them.

Permafrost

The term 'permafrost' is used to describe the way in which the ground in some polar and alpine regions remains permanently frozen.

The strict definition of a permafrost is that it must remain frozen for more than two years without thawing.

There are various different categories of permafrost. The most persistent kind is known as 'cold permafrost'. This remains well below freezing point and so can tolerate significant heating without thawing. On the other hand, 'warm permafrost' is ground that is only just below 0°C (32°F), and so thaws easily on exposure to warmth.

'Ice-rich permafrost' is ground that is composed of more than 20 per cent ice, while 'thaw-stable permafrost' is where the underlying substrate is largely unaffected if a thaw occurs, and is typically made up of bedrock or coarse rock masses. Conversely, ground that is considered to be 'thaw-unstable permafrost' may undergo significant subsidence if it thaws out; thin soils and clays fall into this category.

Although most permafrost areas have seen little change in hundreds of years, global warming has caused many of them to begin thawing out. The most worrying example is that of western Siberia, where 1,000,000km²/621,000mi² of permafrost is melting for the first time in over 10,000 years.

Pesticides

Pesticides are chemicals that are used for agricultural, industrial and domestic purposes to control various animal pests, such as mosquitoes, slugs, snails, caterpillars and cockroaches.

Those chemicals that are specifically targeted towards the control of insects are referred to as insecticides. These products may be derived from natural sources or they may be entirely synthetic.

Some are extremely toxic, not only to the creatures they are aimed at, but also to humans and the wider environment, if used carelessly. A classic example of this is a man-made insecticide known as DDT (from its trivial name Dichloro-Diphenyl-Trichloroethane), developed in the late 1930s. While it proved to be a very effective pesticide, especially in the control of mosquitoes and body lice,

DDT caused all manner of problems, as it tends to build up in the body tissues of creatures such as insect-eating birds. When these are eaten by predators, such as Peregrine Falcons, the chemical build-up can weaken or kill them.

These creatures often stayed in the environment for prolonged periods and killed or weakened more or less every organism they came into contact with. Fortunately, such materials are banned in most countries these days, and are regulated in most of the others. In their place, a variety of more environmentally friendly pesticides have been developed, although these also require responsible use if they are to avoid causing problems for the wider ecosystem.

Pests

In its simplest sense, a pest is an animal that causes some form of problem for humankind. The term 'pest' can also be extended to cover organisms like bacteria and fungi, and even certain plants.

Some of the better-known pests include such creatures as mosquitoes, flies, cockroaches, aphids, termites, fleas, lice, mice, rats and rabbits.

Some creatures are labelled pests because of the things that they consume. Rabbits, for instance, cause enormous amounts of damage to crops and gardens around the world.

The behaviour of other pests may have much more serious implications, however. Being bitten by a mosquito can be unpleasant enough, but many species also transmit potentially fatal diseases such as malaria, dengue fever and yellow fever. Likewise, rats not only do a lot of physical damage to stored food and commercial products, but can also carry a lethal bacteria causing leptospirosis (also known as Weil's disease) which can be fatal.

Rat fleas can carry a variety of extremely dangerous pathogens, including those responsible for bubonic plague. More commonly known as the Black Death, the bubonic plague was a pandemic that spread westwards from Asia to the Atlantic coasts of Europe in the mid 14th century. At the time, around 75 million people were killed.

Such pests continue to cost the global economy incalculable amounts of money every year, both in terms of the damage they do and the costs involved in trying to control them.

See: *Native vs Introduced Species,* page 130

Phytoplankton

Phytoplankton are tiny marine plants that are found in all the world's seas and oceans, many occurring in unimaginable numbers.

Phytoplankton are photosynthetic, using green-coloured chlorophyll pigments in the same manner as other plants to convert sunlight into energy.

These microscopic organisms are one of the primary building blocks of the entire marine environment, and, as a result of their abundance, a wide variety of animals has evolved to feed on them.

At the smaller end of the scale, such creatures include barnacles and larval crustaceans. These are then eaten by small fish, sea anemones and jellyfish, which, in turn, are consumed by bigger fish and other predators. Some whales even feed directly on phytoplankton.

When their numbers drop significantly, this can cause massive fluctuations in the populations of all the species that rely on them. This effect is seen whenever an El Niño event occurs, as the inherent increases in sea surface temperatures prevent deep-water nutrients from reaching the upper levels. Since phytoplankton rely on these, they are unable to survive and their numbers crash. Phytoplankton are therefore important environmental indicators.

One of the most significant aspects of the phytoplankton is their ability to soak up atmospheric carbon dioxide. The extent to which they are able to do this is limited, however, by the supply of nutrients.

See: *Carbon Monoxide & Carbon Dioxide,* page 40; *El Niño,* page 74

Plants

The plant kingdom is one of the main groups of life forms; it covers everything from microscopic algae to flowering plants and trees.

The exact number of different species within the plant kingdom is not known and new varieties are being identified on a regular basis. However, there may be as many as 400,000 different species.

The most numerous family is the orchid, consisting of around 25,000 different species. Others include daisies (around 20,000 species), legumes (16,000 species), madders (13,000 species) and grasses (9,000 species).

It is believed that flowering plants first evolved around 130 million years ago, although non-flowering terrestrial plants (which reproduced with spores) first arose some 300 million years before that. The coralline algae, for example, date from the Cambrian Period, some 450 million years ago.

Most plants use green pigments, called chlorophyll, to convert sunlight into energy, in a process called photosynthesis. Although the leaves of plants are hard to digest and provide relatively small amounts of nourishment, they are the main dietary constituents of many herbivorous animals, including cows, sheep and deer, as well as vast numbers of insects and other invertebrates.

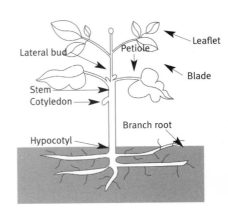

Pollen Count

Pollen is a substance that is produced by all flowering plants as part of the reproductive cycle.

Pollen is composed of minute particles that are released into the air and then transported to new locations by the wind.

Although this is a perfectly natural process that has been occurring for more than 100 million years, certain kinds of pollen can cause very severe allergic reactions in some humans. This is variously known as 'hay fever' or 'rose fever', and is a form of rhinitis, a reaction that occurs in the eyes, nose and throat when airborne irritants or allergens trigger the release of a chemical called 'histamine'. It causes inflammation and fluid production in the delicate linings of the nasal passages, sinuses and eyelids. Hayfever season is usually at its height during May and June.

The amount of pollen in the air is therefore of great significance to sufferers, and so is regularly monitored by most meteorological organizations. The level of airborne allergenic pollen is commonly quoted during weather forecasts, using an indexing system called the pollen count. The type and quantity of pollen varies with the time of year – it rises in the spring, but usually peaks in early summer.

Precipitation

*'Precipitation' is the name given to any kind of moisture
that falls from the air onto the Earth's surface.*

Rain, snow, sleet and hail are all various types of precipitation, but fog and mist are not classed in this way.

Precipitation begins to form when atmospheric water vapour accumulates on a microscopic particle called a condensation nucleus. This is usually composed of a tiny piece of dust, soot, salt or smoke. Once the process has begun, more and more water vapour collects on it and eventually a small droplet forms.

When this gets to about 1mm/0.04in in diameter, it usually coalesces with others and a full-size raindrop develops. When this gets too heavy to remain suspended in the air, gravity takes over and it falls to Earth.

Often the temperature is so low at this stage that it is frozen. On contact with warm air, however, it may thaw out as it falls, so that by the time it reaches the ground it is liquid again.

Meteorologists and hydrologists record the amount of precipitation that falls using rain gauges. There are many different types of these, with some being specifically designed for places that receive a great deal of snow.

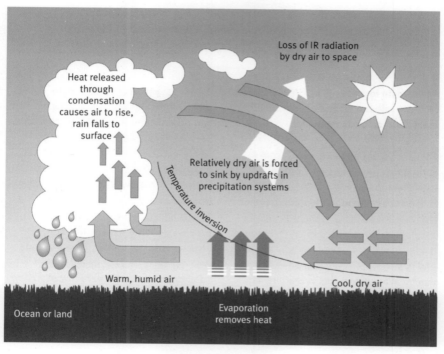

How precipitation occurs.

PVC

PVC, which is short for polyvinyl chloride, is an industrial thermoplastic that is widely used in industry for construction and the manufacture of various goods.

The main ingredients in PVC are derived from salt and oil and are combined to make vinyl chloride monomer.

This is polymerised into a PVC resin that is then tailored to its final application with the addition of certain additives. PVC can be manipulated into more or less any shape using standard extrusion, moulding and thermoforming techniques. It can also be softened to produce fabrics and is also waterproof and an excellent electrical insulator. This versatility has made it one of the chemical industry's most commercially important products.

PVC has, in recent years, more or less replaced the likes of wood, clay, concrete and other traditional building materials, because it is cheap, hard-wearing and easily-put-together. Although this has reduced the need to cut down hardwood trees, PVC is still an undesirable material from an environmental perspective. This is because the manufacturing process generates many harmful atmospheric pollutants. These include dioxins, which, it is believed, are carcinogenic, even at very low exposure levels, and have been linked to several immunological and fertility disorders.

Radioactive Waste

Radioactive waste is created as a by-product of various commercial activities.

By far the largest source of radioactive waste is the nuclear power industry, which produces all manner of contaminated materials.

Those substances containing significant amounts of radioactive chemicals are usually referred to as high-level wastes. These are the most dangerous and so need to be handled and disposed of with considerable care.

Less toxic are low-level wastes and include protective overalls and gloves worn by people who work in the nuclear industry. Typically, all such materials are buried in disused mineshafts, which are then, in turn, sealed with concrete.

For many years it was not unusual for radioactive wastes to be allowed to escape into the environment at research facilities and power stations. Consequently, large areas of land were contaminated, particularly in the countries of the former Soviet Union and the United States.

The process of cleaning up these sites is known as remediation and this is is an enormously expensive exercise. The United States aims to have cleared all its contaminated land within 20 years but, unfortunately, the prohibitive cost is preventing much being done in Russia and many eastern European countries.

See: *Nuclear Power,* page 137

Rainbow

A rainbow is an optical effect in the form of an arc of concentric coloured bands that occurs when the Sun shines through moisture-laden air.

In order to see the rainbow effect clearly, the Sun must be behind or to the side of the observer.

The colours are generated by the way the Sun's light is refracted as it passes through the millions of tiny water drops that are suspended in moisture-rich air. This may be high in the sky as the result of low clouds, or it may be at a much lower level, due to low-lying mist or the spray from features such as large waterfalls.

The longer wavelengths found at the red end of the spectrum hardly deviate at all, but the blue colours at the other end are significantly bent. This causes the primary colours to be separated out as the spectrum of colours that we see as a rainbow. These can be seen as relatively distinct bands of red, orange, yellow, green, blue, indigo and violet.

Sometimes two or more rainbows can be seen in a concentric manner – that is, one inside the other. These are, in fact, not two separate rainbows, but the same one reflected one or more times. Although a secondary rainbow has the same colours as the first (or primary) arc, it has the order reversed.

Recycling

Recycling is the process of taking used items and either reusing them in their existing form, or breaking them up into their constituent parts and then reusing them in some way.

Examples of recycling processes include grinding up car tyres to make soft ground coverings for children's playgrounds, or melting down old glass bottles to make new ones.

There are many potential benefits to recycling. For a start, it cuts down on the need for waste disposal, reduces the need to extract raw materials and lowers the amount of pollutants reaching the environment.

There is usually also a marked saving in energy when recycling, both in terms of transportation costs as well as in the manufacturing process.

Recycling has become a major industry in the last 20 years or so, and most developed countries have well-organized collection systems for all manner of materials, including paper, glass, aluminium, iron, fabrics, plastics and vegetative waste.

Many places have strict laws to ensure that both domestic and commercial wastes are handled efficiently. One of the main issues is in ensuring that people who are disposing of their recyclable wastes take the trouble to properly sort them out – this saves time, money, and ultimately benefits both humankind and the environment.

Renewable Energy

The term 'renewable energy' refers to sources of power that do not rely on fossil fuels.

The wind, tides, Sun, flowing water and nuclear power are all examples of sources of renewable energy.

One of the problems associated with harnessing them is that it can cost more in energy terms to make the necessary equipment and transport it to its working location than the resultant device will ever make.

In many ways, nuclear power is the cleanest and most efficient solution, but there are too many downsides for it to become a politically acceptable solution, at least until the technology improves.

Wind power went out of vogue with the coming of electricity, but large turbines are now an increasingly common feature of many landscapes across the world.

While solar panels are a good way of harnessing the Sun's energy to heat water in hot countries, they are not currently a very efficient means of generating electricity. This situation is likely to change in the near future, though, thanks to recent advances in photovoltaic cell technology. If all goes well, this will not only improve the output of solar panels, but will also reduce their cost to more economically viable levels.

Many countries now generate significant amounts of their electrical needs from hydroelectric or tidal power schemes. While these are clean and quiet, the construction of special reservoirs to feed generators can have deleterious consequences for the environment.

See: *Wind Power*, page 202

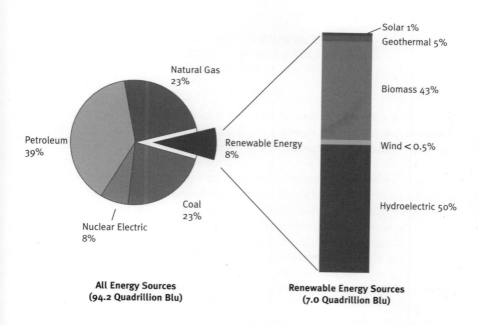

Solar 1%
Geothermal 5%

Natural Gas
23%

Biomass 43%

Petroleum
39%

Renewable Energy
8%

Wind < 0.5%

Coal
23%

Hydroelectric 50%

Nuclear Electric
8%

All Energy Sources
(94.2 Quadrillion Blu)

Renewable Energy Sources
(7.0 Quadrillion Blu)

Approximate percentage of total energy provided from renewable energy sources.

Reptiles

Found on every continent apart from Antarctica, reptiles are vertebrate animals that belong to the class Sauropsida.

Reptiles are divided into four distinct orders which, together, number more than 8,000 different species.

The four orders of reptiles consist of Squamata, which includes snakes and lizards; Crocodilia, such as crocodiles and alligators; Spenodontia, including tuataras; and Testudines, such as turtles and tortoises. The most numerous by far are the snakes and lizards of the Squamata category, which has around 7,900 species.

Reptiles are 'ectothermic', which means that they are unable to generate their own body heat, and have to rely on their environment to maintain their body temperatures. In practice, this usually means that when they are cold they have to bask in the Sun in order to absorb sufficient heat to make their muscles work properly.

Conversely, when they get too hot, they have to find a suitable way of cooling down. Usually, this means either going down a cool hole or diving into water.

Most reptiles feed on small creatures, such as insects, frogs and mice, but others – such as tortoises – are exclusively herbivorous. The bigger ones, however, can consume large prey. Crocodiles, alligators and Komodo Dragons, for example, can kill and eat goats, cows and, sometimes, even humans.

See: *Herbivores*, page 106

Reservoirs

Reservoirs are human-made lakes that are used to store water for domestic, agricultural and/or industrial purposes.

Reservoirs are often used to power hydroelectric schemes and are therefore especially popular in developing countries where there are often insufficient local reserves of coal or oil.

Constructing a reservoir usually involves the flooding of large areas of virgin land and this destroys all the habitats that they cover. This is particularly bad for the environment, as the places that are lost are typically the most biodiverse in the affected region.

The construction phase begins with the establishment of the foundations for a dam, after which vast quantities of rock, soil or concrete are built up until the required height is achieved. The flooding process then begins, but since the chosen sites are usually centred on sheltered valleys, these are often home to indigenous tribespeople. As a result, such people are permanently displaced from their home territories.

Once the dam is built, it still has a negative impact on the environment, especially for the downstream aquatic habitats. Changes in water flow, temperature and quality can easily lead to the endangerment or extinction of many of the plants and animals that live there.

Rivers

Rivers are large waterways that lead from inland areas to the sea.

As home to huge numbers of plants and animals, as well as natural distributors of irrigation for lowland areas, rivers are tremendously important to the environment.

Typically, rivers arise in highland areas as the result of the accumulation of precipitated water (and these are known as catchment areas). This water may be brought to the surface from underground sources or it may come from a pond or upland bog; alternatively, it may be from glacial meltwaters.

At this stage, the water may be just a trickle, but as it runs downhill, its flow increases as other trickles combine with it, eventually forming a stream.

In undisturbed areas, these shallow waterways are used as breeding grounds by many species of fish – especially salmon – as well as amphibians and large numbers of aquatic invertebrates.

As the river gets closer to the sea it usually grows significantly larger as other waterways join it. Eventually, it reaches the sea, either directly or via a tidal estuary.

Rivers are threatened by a number of environmental factors. Pollution, from domestic or industrial sources, is very high on the list, along with habitat loss or disturbance along the margins, as the result of various human activities.

Saffir–Simpson Hurricane Scale

This index is used to categorize the strength of hurricanes.

The Saffir–Simpson Hurricane Scale was formulated in 1969 by Herbert Saffir and Bob Simpson.

The scale relates the maximum sustained wind speeds of a given level of storm to the amount of damage that they are likely to cause. It is exclusively used in the Atlantic and Pacific Oceans. Different methods of measurement are used in other parts of the world.

THE SAFFIR–SIMPSON HURRICANE SCALE (SSHS)
CATEGORY ONE (WEAK): Winds 74–95mph/119–152kph or storm surge 4–5ft/1.2–1.5m above normal *Little effect on buildings, but extensive damage to mobile homes and trees possible.*
CATEGORY TWO (MODERATE): Winds 96–110mph/154–177kph or storm surge 6–8ft/1.8–2.4m above normal *Damage primarily to mobile homes, piers and vegetation; coastal areas flooded.*
CATEGORY THREE (STRONG): Winds 111–130mph/178–209kph or storm surge 9–12ft/2.7–3.6m above normal *Damage to small houses, mobile homes destroyed; large-scale coastal flooding.*
CATEGORY FOUR (VERY STRONG): Winds 131–155mph/210–249kph or storm surge 13–18ft/3.9–5.4m above normal *Major damage to large buildings; entire roofs destroyed. Severe coastal flooding; significant beach erosion.*
CATEGORY FIVE (DEVASTATING): Winds greater than 155mph/249kph or storm surge greater than 18ft/5.4m above normal *Industrial buildings may be badly damaged; smaller ones destroyed. Wide-scale evacuation for up to 10 miles/16.09 km inland.*

Saltwater Intrusion

Saltwater intrusion is a process whereby saline water from the sea makes its way inland and contaminates freshwater sources such as ponds, streams, marshes, canals and rivers.

Saltwater intrusion can be a result of natural events, such as hurricanes and tsunamis, which can force large quantities of sea water overland and into nearby areas over a matter of a few hours.

It can also occur more slowly as the result of underground seepage. Normally, this movement is counterbalanced by the outflow of water, in the opposite direction, from high ground.

Where humankind is extracting significant quantities of water for domestic, agricultural or industrial purposes, however, this balance can be upset and salt may penetrate much further inland than usual. It can leach into the ground, making it impossible for the native vegetation to survive.

This can have very serious consequences for the environment, as it can endanger entire ecosystems, especially where the soil relies on plant roots for stability. Rapid erosion can occur when the vegetation dies. In extreme cases the salt levels may get so high that traditional supplies of water for towns and cities become unusable.

Even if the local water extraction is halted, the problem does not go away as the ground is still laden with salt. One solution is to use salt-tolerant plants as a form of bioremediation. It is a long process, however, and in most cases is too expensive to consider.

Savannahs

The word 'savannah' comes from the Spanish term for 'treeless plain'.

The original definition for the term 'savannah' is: *'an open tropical grassland that is more or less entirely covered with low vegetation'*. **These days, however, the label is sometimes used for areas that also support scrub bushes and small trees.**

Savannahs are mostly found between the latitudes of 25° S and 25° N, where there is enough rainfall to sustain desert grasses, but insufficient for trees to survive. Often, the precipitation only occurs for a few months of the year in a marked wet season, and typical annual figures are in the range of between 100mm and 400mm (4 and 16in).

In some areas, though, the rainfall is higher, but forests are unable to form because of grazing by animals, a lack of soil or the occurrence of frequent wildfires.

Savannahs are found in parts of India, Indochina, West Africa, Southern Africa, South America and much of the northern Australian coast. Similar landscapes are also seen in cooler climates, but these are termed 'dry grasslands'.

In the dry seasons there is little to eat or drink, whereas the opposite is true in the wet seasons. In order to deal with this, the animals that populate savannahs have evolved to cope with these large variations in climate in one of two ways: they either migrate, or keep their populations low enough for sustenance to be possible throughout the year.

See: *Grasslands*, page 98

Scrubbers

Scrubbers are devices that are installed in the exhaust outlets of various industrial facilities to remove or neutralize certain atmospheric pollutants.

The pollutants that scrubbers deal with may be in the form of microscopic particulates or harmful gases such as sulphur dioxide and hydrochloric acid.

There are two basic forms of such devices – 'wet' and 'dry' scrubbers. Wet scrubbing works by using a liquid to trap the unwanted components by direct contact with them. Where these are simple dust particles, for example, the liquid used may simply be water, but for more noxious substances, a special solution is usually employed.

Often the output of the chimneys concerned may appear to the uninitiated to be worse than before the scrubber was fitted. However, this is because large amounts of water vapour are released and this is much more visible to the naked eye than the dangerous pollutants which are generally invisible.

Dry scrubbers use specially formulated powders or gases that, as the name would suggest, do not contain significant amounts of water. As a result, the output plumes from the chimneys are far less noticeable, making them more popular from the perspective of the local population.

They are much more expensive to install and maintain, however, and so can only be implemented where there are sufficient resources to pay for them. As a result, dry scrubbers are rarely used in developing countries.

Sea Level

The world's sea levels have received a significant amount of attention in recent years, as the result of changes brought about by global warming.

———————

As the polar ice caps melt, the amount of water in the oceans increases, raising their average levels.

The rise in sea levels caused by melting ice caps is exacerbated by the fact that water expands as it gets hotter. It should be noted, though, that alterations in the amount of floating pack ice do not contribute to this, as it displaces the same volume whether it is in solid or liquid form.

Such changes have, however, occurred since before life itself evolved on Earth. Scientists have established that the sea is almost as low now as it has ever been, and that in the last 100 million years, it was lowest at the peak of the last ice age, around 20,000 years ago. At this time, it was about 130m/400ft below its current level. These days, it is thought that they are rising by about 3mm/0.1in a year, and that the rate is increasing.

One interesting source of evidence for rises in sea level over the last 250 years is shown in the art works of the Italian painter Canaletto (Giovanni Antonio Canal, 1697–1768) . The artist's famous depictions of his native Venice are considered accurate enough to determine how high the spring tides rose in the early 18th century, providing valuable clues as to how sea levels may change in the near future.

Exactly what will happen in the future remains unclear, however. Some climatologists' projections suggest that many low-lying areas will be inundated within the next few decades.

See: *Glaciers*, page 94

Smog

*Short for 'smoke fog', smog is a
type of atmospheric pollution.*

Smog is formed when conventional
fog is contaminated by airborne
pollutants, such as sulphur and fluorine
compounds, as well as hydrochloric
acid and carbon dioxide.

When all these components are mixed up
in a damp atmosphere, the air becomes
highly toxic to most forms of life, including
humans. Sometimes local weather
conditions can cause particularly bad
incidents – the worst being an event that
began in London on 4 December 1952. In
those days, there were few regulations
about what people were allowed to burn
and, as a result, industrial and domestic
chimneys poured out massive quantities
of harmful smoke.

On this occasion, a low-pressure
centre settled over the area, trapping
all the pollutants for five days, and
several thousand people lost their lives.
However, following a public outcry, new
laws were quickly passed in an attempt
to prevent such a catastrophe from ever
happening again.

These actions were largely successful
in the United Kingdom, although many
developing countries, especially in
Southeast Asia, still have big smog
problems due to the amount of forest-
burning taking place in those areas.

See: *Forests*, pages 84–85

Snow

Snow is a form of precipitation that is made up of large numbers of tiny ice crystals that have coalesced into flakes.

When the air is cold enough, snowflakes reach the ground without melting, and if conditions are suitable, they will accumulate to a depth that is around ten times that of an equivalent rain shower.

In temperate regions, however, the ground temperatures are often too high for this to happen except in the depths of winter, and most or all of the snow melts soon after landing.

Light falls are described as flurries, but heavier ones are known as squalls. Long-duration snowstorms are referred to as blizzards and are often accompanied by strong winds, which can blow the snow for considerable distances. This produces drifts that can be many times deeper than the overall covering, and can block roads, railways and footpaths, causing all manner of problems for local people.

The highest recorded fall of snow took place in Silver Lake, Colorado, USA, in 1921, when 1.93m/76in fell in just one single day.

When snow falls in particularly cold places it may persist throughout the summer. If this happens for many years in a row, it can accumulate to such an extent that its own weight compacts the lower layers into ice.

When the weight of the ice is sufficient to overcome the ground's friction, the ice will start to flow and a glacier is formed.

See: *Glaciers*, page 94; *Precipitation*, pages 152–153

Soil Erosion

Soil erosion is the removal of surface material from the ground.

Surface material is removed from the ground via the action of strong winds, heavy rainfall, the movement of ice, the feet of humans and animals or, quite often, a combination of several of these factors.

From an environmental perspective, soil erosion is frequently caused by poor land-management techniques. Slash-and-burn agriculture is a classic example of this, occuring when peasant farmers cut down and burn virgin forest and then plant their own crops in the resulting open spaces.

In such situations, the soil is very thin and so it can only sustain the growth of one or two seasons before all its nutrients have been used up. The farmers then move on and destroy a new section of forest in the same way. The abandoned land, however, is soon washed away as there is no vegetation to bind it in place.

On steep landscapes this often happens without warning in the form of a sudden landslide and, tragically, many people all over the world have been killed in this way.

The remaining ground is left as bare bedrock and the washed-out soil tends to silt up nearby waterways. These are both catastrophic events for local ecosystems.

See: *Agriculture*, page 9

Soil Fertility

Soil fertility is a measure of the ability of a given piece of ground to support plant and animal life.

Soil fertility is environmentally significant: many ancient ecosystems, for example, are established on soils that have a naturally low fertility. If these are 'improved' through the use of additional fertilizers, the plants that were formerly able to maintain a hold there are almost always quickly displaced by others.

In such a case the endangerment or loss of sensitive species may result. Slash-and-burn farming can also reduce soil fertility to the point where no vegetation can survive. This can leave vast areas of once fertile land exposed to severe erosion. The soil that has been washed away may accumulate in local waterways, blocking them and killing many plants and animals in the process.

Alternatively, the overuse of fertilizers is also detrimental to the environment, resulting in large amounts of nitrates being washed into waterways and out to sea, and causing algal blooms that starve the waters of oxygen and block out sunlight, killing more or less all the resident organisms. Some experts believe this has also caused the death of many coral reefs.

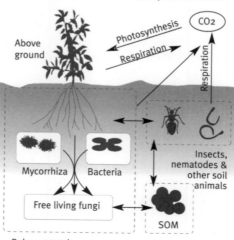

Solar Power

Solar power is energy that is obtained in some manner from the Sun.

About one-fifth of the Sun's energy is absorbed by the atmosphere, and just over a third is reflected back into space by clouds.

The rest – between 125 and 375w/m² (watts per square metre) – in temperate areas actually reaches the ground. Plants exploit this by using chlorophyll pigments to convert sunlight into energy in a process called photosynthesis.

Without sufficient light their leaves turn pale and eventually die. Many animals, especially reptiles and amphibians, are unable to generate their own heat and depend entirely on the Sun to keep their bodies warm.

Humans have also devised a number of methods of capturing and using sunlight – typically, large panels are used to heat water or generate electricity. One of the most common methods of doing this is to use 'photovoltaic' or 'photoelectric' cells. These are specialized semiconductors that turn sunlight into weak electric currents. Currently, this method is expensive and inefficient, but advances in technology are likely to make it more viable within a few years.

Many hot countries use solar collectors to heat water, which is then stored in large tanks for later use. It is one of the most environmentally friendly forms of energy as, once installed, no greenhouse gases are released. This means that significant financial savings can be made, thereby reducing demands on the local economy.

See: *Greenhouse Effect*, page 99; *Sun*, page 178

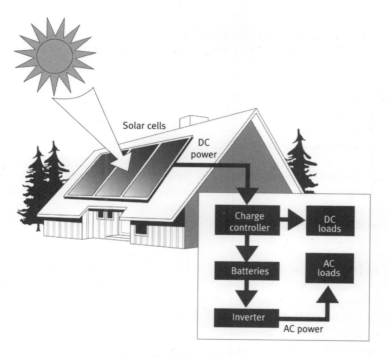

Solar cells

DC power

Charge controller → DC loads

Batteries

AC loads

Inverter — AC power

The creation of solar power.

Steppe

The steppe is a semi-arid climate region that is characterized by extensive grasslands.

Steppes are only found in the interiors of the North American and Eurasian continents where wet air from the oceans is blocked by mountain ranges.

Steppe landscapes therefore have low annual precipitation, varying between 10cm and 50cm (4 and 20in), depending on the location. They are highly dependent on this remaining relatively constant from year to year. If the figure drops too far the grasses cannot survive and if it increases significantly, they are replaced by more vigorous species.

The steppe climate is one of great extremes. In the summer temperatures may climb to 40°C (104°F), whereas in the depths of winter they may fall to -40°C (-40°F).

The main steppes are found between the latitudes of 35° and 55° N. One stretches across the Great Basin, the Columbia Plateau and the Great Plains of western North America, and the other is found in vast swathes that spread from eastern Europe to the Gobi Desert and northern China.

The steppes are home to many plants and animals that are found nowhere else. These include certain species of lynx, antelope, rodents, birds, sagebrush and other small shrubs. These organisms are increasingly vulnerable to the climatic changes brought about by global warming, especially as large areas have already been converted into agricultural land. As a result, the remaining pockets urgently need conserving.

See: *Grasslands*, page 98; *Savannahs*, page 165

Stratosphere

The stratosphere is an atmospheric layer that is separated from the troposphere by the tropopause.

The stratosphere extends from around 10 to 50km (6 to 31mi) above the ground. Its lower boundary varies depending on latitude, with it being higher at the equator than the poles.

The air in this zone is relatively dry and the only significant clouds are found in the lower regions. These include cirrus, cirrostratus and cirrocumulus types.

The ozone layer is found in the mid-stratosphere, at an altitude of about 25 km/15.5mi. This absorbs most of the ultraviolet components in the Sun's radiation and, in so doing, warms the air around it significantly.

This situation leads the temperature to increase with elevation, rising from about -55°C (-67°F) at its lowest point to about 0°C (32°F) in the upper reaches.

The winds found in the stratosphere tend to flow horizontally and are both much more stable and predictable than those found at lower altitudes. The air is also thinner than that at lower altitudes and, as a result, most commercial airliners fly in this layer as it is smoother for the passengers. An added advantage of doing this is that it also saves fuel.

Above the stratosphere is the mesosphere, with the two being separated by the stratopause.

See: *Ozone Layer*, page 143

Sulphur Dioxide

Sulphur dioxide (SO$_2$) is a toxic gas that is released into the atmosphere as a result of various domestic, industrial and geologic activities.

Sulphur dioxide (SO$_2$) is produced when sulphur is burned in the presence of oxygen and, as this is found in coal and oil, large quantities of sulphur dioxide are generated by the combustion of fossil fuels, especially by power stations and motor vehicles.

When sulphur dioxide comes into contact with damp air, an acidic solution is created. This is then usually converted into acidic sulphates (SO$_4^2$) by the energy contained in sunlight and contact with catalytic agents, such as certain nitric oxides.

Consequently, any precipitation that is formed in the vicinity has the capacity to seriously damage plant and aquatic life,

as well as cause health problems for animals, including humans.

Many developed countries have gone to considerable lengths to reduce their output of sulphur dioxide with the use of exhaust scrubbers and other technologies such as low sulphur gasoline and diesel. Others, such as India and China, either have no regulations in place or have failed to enforce the ones that they do have. As a result, these countries continue to pour millions of tons of sulphur-bearing chemicals into the atmosphere every year, mostly from the chimneys of coal-fired power stations. This disparity is the cause of significant tension in political circles.

See: *Scrubbers*, page 166

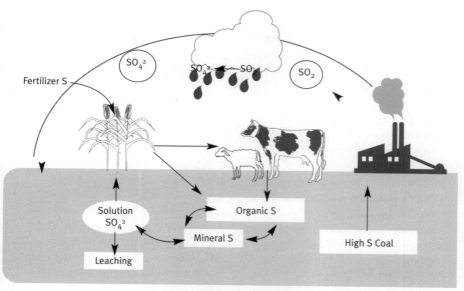

How sulphur dioxide (SO₂) is produced.

Sun

*The Sun is an enormous ball of hot gases.
It is so vast that more than a million planets
the size of Earth could fit inside it.*

Measuring about 1,392,140km/ 865,059mi across, the sun is mainly composed of hydrogen (70 per cent), plus helium (28 per cent), carbon (1.5 per cent), nitrogen and oxygen, as well as a few other minor components.

Despite being comprised of these lightweight gases, it still makes up about 99.8 per cent of the Solar System's total mass.

The Sun is a long way from the Earth, being, on average, about 149,668,992km/ 93,000,000mi away. At this distance, the light it produces takes eight and a half minutes to reach us. This sunlight is responsible for the existence of all life on Earth, and is produced as a by-product of the fierce combustion that permanently rages across its surface.

The temperature there is around 5,537°C (10,000°F), but at the centre this rises to 499,998°C (27,000,000°F). This produces a wide spectrum of powerful electromagnetic radiation, and if most of this was not filtered out by the Earth's atmosphere, life as we know it could not exist. This is one of the reasons why it is so important that the release of atmospheric pollutants is minimized, especially those which damage the ozone layer.

See: *Ozone Layer*, page 143; *Sunspots*, page 179

Sunspots

Sunspots are areas on the Sun's surface where the gases are at significantly lower temperatures than those around them.

The temperatures within sunspots are usually around 5,000°C (9,000°F), compared with the more usual level of 5,540°C (10,000°F).

Sunspots can be easily observed using simple pinhole camera systems that safely project an image of the Sun onto a piece of card. The spots then show up as small dark areas on the Sun's surface.

For reasons that are still not fully understood, sunspots are responsible for the emission of intense magnetic fields. These carry so much energy that they can knock out communications systems on Earth, and have occasionally even disabled power generation networks.

They are also a great danger to satellites. Scientists working with ice core samples have recently discovered that over the last 60 years the Sun has been more active than for the previous 8,000 years. Whether this is actually responsible for global warming rather than humankind's activities is still a matter of fierce debate.

The evidence, however, suggests that there is a direct correlation between the presence of sunspots and the Earth's average temperature. In the late 17th and early 18th centuries, for example, there were very few sunspots, coinciding with a long period of cold weather known as the 'Little Ice Age'.

See: *Global Warming*, pages 96–97; *Sun*, page 178

Sustainable Use

This is an eminently practical philosophy whereby the exploitation of any natural resource is performed in such a way that it will last indefinitely.

In the modern world, most of our resources are at a premium because fossil fuels are running out, and so the concept of 'sustainable use' has risen to prominence in recent years.

An example of this concept is that trees can be harvested for use by the timber industry in a sustainable manner if the right species are grown in the right way, and new ones are grown to replace any that are felled.

Likewise, the fishing industry could also be made to work in a sustainable manner if it was managed properly. Unfortunately, it can be very difficult to get the various nations that fish a given area to agree as to exactly how such measures should be implemented. As a result, the regulations required to make such policies workable often stall in the discussion stage, and so little or nothing gets done.

The generation of electricity can also be sustainable, and this may be achieved in a number of ways. The most efficient form is nuclear power, although this is not a popular choice with many people. Wind turbines, solar panels and hydroelectric schemes are all sustainable methods, and when done properly they can work well.

For sustainable use to be successful though, it needs both political will and societal support. It also needs good management, adequate funding and efficient implementation, however.

See: *Extinction*, page 79; *Fishing*, page 80; *Nuclear Power*, page 137; *Solar Power*, page 172–173; *Wind Power*, page 202

Taiga

Also known as boreal forests, taigas are predominantly coniferous habitats that are found at sub-polar latitudes of between 50°–70° North and South.

The proximity of taigas to the poles results in extreme temperature variations, ranging from around -25°C (-14°F) during the long, harsh winters, to highs of about 20°C (70°F) in the short, mild summers.

Typically, taigas are only free of frost for two to three months of the year. Taigas can be found on the North American continent, distributed across central and western Alaska, from the Yukon Territory to Labrador in Canada. In Eurasia, they occur across northern Europe and Siberia, running as far east as the Pacific Ocean.

Most of the animals that live in these places either move to warmer climates or hibernate during the colder months.

In the summer, the air is often thick with biting insects and many different species of birds migrate to the taigas in order to breed. Large animals inhabiting these areas include deer, moose and elk, as well as predators such as wolves and lynx.

The vegetation growing in taigas is limited to a small number of flowering plants as well as various grasses, lichens and mosses, because of the often extreme climate.

See: *Forests*, page 84–85; *Grasslands*, page 98; *Savannahs*, page 165

Temperate Rainforest

Temperate rainforests are only found in mid-latitude areas where precipitation is high enough for trees to grow in profusion. This is generally above 1.2m/4ft a year, although in some regions it may be significantly higher.

There are three different kinds of temperate rainforest: deciduous, evergreen, and mixed evergreen/deciduous rainforests, and each has its own characteristic range of fauna and flora.

Deciduous rainforests have the greatest biodiversity and are usually made up of a wide variety of broadleaf trees that, in turn, support many animals – from tiny invertebrates through to large mammals and birds.

Conversely, evergreen forests only have a small number of coniferous species. They usually include hemlock, pine, spruce and fir. In the southern hemisphere eucalyptus trees may also grow in these forests.

Temperate rainforests used to cover vast areas of the mid-latitudes, but mankind has since cut most of them down for timber or to make way for agriculture. This process started not long after the end of the last Ice Age, with the pace of destruction reaching a peak in the 20th century.

Currently, temperate rainforests only cover about half of their original extent. Some of the largest expanses of temperate rainforests are found in the Pacific Northwest, from the coasts of Washington and along the borders of Canada as far as Alaska.

See: *Forests*, page 84–85

Thermosphere

The thermosphere is the outermost atmospheric layer of the Earth and is often referred to as the 'upper atmosphere'.

Lying above the mesosphere, this layer also includes the ionosphere. Overall, it is a vast zone that extends from about 80km/50mi above the ground to an altitude of around 640km/400mi.

In the thermosphere, the air is extremely thin, however, and is therefore easily heated by solar radiation. The temperature increases with elevation, and in the upper levels reaches around 1,700°C (3,060°F). When the Sun is particularly active this may rise as high as 2,500°C (4,500°F).

In the ionosphere the heat is sufficient to cause some molecules to ionise. This results in the layer being filled with charged particles.

Despite the air in the thermosphere being very thin, it filters out all the X-rays as well as the most dangerous forms of ultraviolet radiation that would otherwise reach the Earth. Without this protection, very little life could exist on our planet.

The auroras – that is, the phenomena commonly known as the Northern Lights and Southern Lights – are formed in the ionosphere as the result of charged particles from the solar wind interacting with those in the atmosphere. When there is a great deal of solar activity, these can form extremely impressive nocturnal flashing light displays in the regions close to the poles at particular times of the year.

See: *Aurora Borealis*, pages 24–25

Thunderstorms

Thunderstorms are weather events during which thunder and lightning are generated.

There are many different types of thunderstorms, including single cell, multicell cluster, multicell lines (squalls) and supercells.

Thunderstorms can only form if there is sufficient moisture in the air, the temperature is high enough for unstable updrafts to form, and something is lifting the air. This lift can be provided by a weather front, a sea breeze, or by the air moving over geophysical features such as mountains.

Single cell thunderstorms are usually very localized, short-lived affairs that last less than an hour. They are very hard to predict, and can deliver strong downbursts as well as hailstorms or weak tornadoes.

Multicell cluster storms, which are the most common types, are made up of several individual storm cells and can produce heavy rainfall, hail, flash floods and weak tornadoes. Multicell line storms are similar, but form in long lines.

The strongest thunderstorms are known as supercells. These can produce severe weather, including heavy rainfall and strong winds. They are sometimes accompanied by large hailstones and less often, spawn violent tornadoes.

Thunderstorms can be very dangerous for aircraft that accidentally stray into them as the mixture of strong updrafts and downdrafts can render flight control impossible. They can also present a real threat to those on the ground unless suitable shelter is available.

See: *Hail*, page 102; *Tornadoes*, page 186

Tidal Power

Tidal power is a form of energy that is extracted from the movements of the tides.

The generation of tidal power is a clean and sustainable practice, as it does not rely on any operational resources and, once installed, does not generate any atmospheric or environmental pollution.

Two main types of tidal power generation are currently available. One exploits differences in the height of water between the high and low tide marks to power electrical generators. This is not a popular method, however, as it depends on special structures such as artificial lagoons or sea dams being built in order to work.

These structures disturb natural habitats and sometimes cause siltation or turbidity problems during the construction phase; they are therefore not at all environmentally friendly.

The other system employs strong marine currents to turn hydroelectric turbines. Since water is both heavy and incompressible, it is much better suited than air to turning turbines and so it can generate a lot more power.

Another significant advantage is that the movements of the sea are well understood and so tidal-powered generators of this type are therefore much more predictable than those which rely on the wind.

This method is therefore much better for the environment than those that rely on lagoons or dams. However, it does require meticulous planning to ensure that the very best sites are chosen.

See: *Habitat*, page 103; *Wind*, page 201;
Wind Power, page 202

Tornadoes

The force of the winds that a tornado creates can wreak havoc on any object with which they come into contact.

A tornado is a violent funnel-shaped wind vortex which forms a rotating column of air from the base of a cumulonimbus cloud during severe thunderstorms. This reaches to the ground, where the force of the winds can be dangerous and destructive.

Tornadoes vary from weak in power – in which the wind speed is less than about 175kph/110mph – to violent, in which the speeds exceed 320kph/200mph.

Although they can occur in many parts of the world, the most notorious region is the United States, where powerful tornadoes form regularly. There is a belt of land that stretches across parts of Texas, Oklahoma, Kansas and Nebraska which suffers from the effects of tornadoes at certain times of the year.

Despite the fact that they are usually associated with severe thunderstorms called supercells, tornadoes also form within hurricanes in such places as the Gulf of Mexico, an area that includes Florida, South Carolina and Georgia.

Waterspouts or sea spouts are basically tornadoes that form over water. Although they are commonly perceived as being phenomena that occur over the oceans, they can also form over large rivers and lakes.

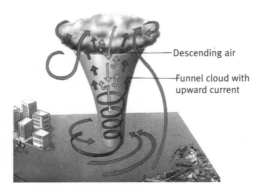

Descending air

Funnel cloud with upward current

Treethanol

The name 'treethanol' has been adopted for a newly developed type of fuel based on ethanol that has been derived from trees.

The technical term for treethanol is 'cellulosic ethanol'. It is chemically identical to ethanol in that it is made from other sources, such as sugar or corn.

With the reduction in the world's fossil-fuel reserves comes an increasing pressure to find new and sustainable alternatives.

Fuels made from maize and sugar cane have been available for years, but have their drawbacks. For a start, they use land that would otherwise be used for growing food crops. This raises the price of many staple foodstuffs and can cause hardship for millions of people.

Ethanol produced from trees does not cause these types of problems, emitting far fewer pollutant gasses than fossil fuels, for example.

The extraction process is also, theoretically, over four times more efficient than that for maize.

The refinement process is, however, still in its infancy, and much work still needs to be done before it becomes readily available. When this happens, it will help the environment in many ways. Ethanol is a much cleaner burning fuel than those derived from oil and a wide variety of suitable trees can be grown in a sustainable manner.

See: *Fossil Fuels*, page 86–87

Tributyltin

Tributyltin (TBT) is a toxic chemical that is used as a biocide – a substance that kills all kinds of organisms.

TBT is found in wood treatments and is an anti-fungal agent in many industrial facilities such as paper mills, textile factories and power plant cooling towers.

Until fairly recently, TBT was also one of the primary constituents in marine anti-fouling materials.

Its use is much more restricted these days. This is because the hulls of boats and ships need to be scraped down regularly and, as a result, flakes of TBT-rich paints began accumulating in harbours and estuaries as well as on the sea bed. It is thought that this was a major factor in the decline of a number of marine organisms, including many species of molluscs such as the Dog Whelk.

Where the levels are not high enough to kill the organism concerned, the presence of this persistent toxin causes a wide variety of reproductive problems. Mammals are also prone to this kind of poisoning. Studies have shown that when dead sea otters and bottlenose dolphins are washed up on the shore, they often have very high levels of TBT in their body tissues.

See: *Molluscs*, page 129

Tropical Rainforests

Rainforests are under pressure from human activities, but they are crucial to the world's climate systems.

Tropical rainforests are found in the zones either side of the equator, between the Tropic of Cancer (23.5° N), and the Tropic of Capricorn (23.5° S), across the continents of America, Africa, and Asia.

The high rainfall that tropical rainforests receive allows trees to grow in profusion, and the forests are usually composed of four distinct layers, all of which can teem with a rich variety of exotic species of plants and animals.

Rainforests are home to two-thirds of all the living animal and plant species on the planet. It has been estimated that many hundreds of millions of new species of plants, insects and microorganisms are still undiscovered and as yet unnamed by science.

Tropical rainforests are also often called the 'Earth's lungs', although there is actually no scientific basis for such a claim, as tropical rainforests are known to be essentially oxygen neutral, with little or no net oxygen production.

The emergent zone is the highest layer in the rainforest, and is formed from the tops of large trees – it is the home of such creatures as parrots and butterflies.

Just below the emergent zone is the upper canopy, where the majority of the rainforest's animals live. The understory is the next layer – this has insufficient light for most plants and animals, and so is the least populated of all the zones.

Although the forest floor receives even less sunlight, it is still home to many animals and fungi, which feed on decaying material falling from the trees.

See: *Climate,* pages 50–51; *Deforestation,* page 64; *Forests,* page 84–85

Troposphere

The troposphere is the layer of the atmosphere that is closest to the surface of the Earth and holds about three-quarters of the world's atmospheric mass.

The depth of the troposphere is thinnest at the poles and thickest over the equator, ranging from about 8–16km/5–10mi deep respectively.

It is composed of nitrogen (78 per cent) and oxygen (21 per cent), with various other gases present in trace quantities, and also contains almost all of the zone's atmospheric moisture.

The air in the troposphere is heated by the ground rather than directly by the Sun and, as a result, its temperature falls as altitude increases – typically, it averages around 17°C (63°F) at the ground, and about -52°C (-62°F) at its highest reaches.

Almost all of the meteorological events that we call weather take place in this layer, with most of them being the direct result of the movements of air caused by the convection currents caused by these temperature differences.

Above the swirling masses of air that make up the troposphere is a much more stable boundary zone, known as the tropopause. At the equator, this typically has a temperature of around -80°C (-112°F) throughout the year, but at the poles, where the layer is much closer to the Earth's surface, it varies between about -40°C (-40°F) in summer and -60°C (-76°F) in winter.

See: *Ozone Layer*, page 143

Tsunami

A tsunami is a wave that is created when a large body of water such as a lake, sea or ocean is subjected to a large impulse.

A tsunami wave is usually the result of an underwater disturbance caused by an earthquake, although it can also be generated by an asteroid impact, volcanic eruption, landslide or any other tumultuous event.

Although tsunamis are often referred to as tidal waves, they do not actually arise from the actions of the tides.

They can vary in magnitude from very small to very large and may cause enormous amounts of damage and claim many lives, or they may simply pass without notice.

Those caused by localized events generally dissipate very quickly, but the ones resulting from major upheavals of the Earth's crust can travel hundreds or even thousands of miles. The 2004 Indian Ocean earthquake was an example of this kind of event, and is believed to have cost well over 220,000 lives and many critical injuries.

Scientists have postulated that tsunamis could form at much bigger scales under certain conditions. These are termed 'mega-tsunamis', and would have the capacity to cause catastrophic damage to entire regions.

How tsunamis work: tsunamigenesis.

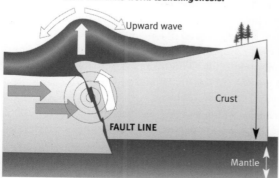

Upward wave

Crust

FAULT LINE

Mantle

Tundras

Tundras are ecosystems that are found in Arctic regions between the latitudes of 60°–75° North, mostly in coastal areas.

Although they typically have long, severe winters, the temperatures they experience – down to around -34°C (-30°F) – are moderated to a certain extent by their proximity to the oceans.

When winter ends there is a short mild season with highs of only 6°C (41°F) or thereabouts before the cold returns. As a result, there is no true spring, summer or autumn.

Tundras receive relatively little in the way of precipitation, with annual figures showing only around 20cm/8in.

This climate produces a harsh environment for animals and plants, with little biodiversity during the cold months.

During the mild period, however, many millions of birds migrate to the area in order to breed, exploiting the vast numbers of insects that swarm over the region to feed their young.

The soil in tundra regions tends to be very shallow and lies on top of permafrost, which significantly reduces the number of plants that can grow on it. Grasses, sedges, lichens and mosses are examples of the predominant species.

Tundras are distributed around the coasts of the northernmost parts of the North American continent, including the Hudson Bay region, the coasts of Greenland, and parts of northern Siberia.

See: *Biodiversity*, page 29; *Climate*, page 20–51; *Grasslands*, page 98; *Permafrost*, page 146

Ultraviolet Radiation

Ultraviolet radiation is a form of electromagnetic energy that is produced by the Sun that cannot be seen by the human eye.

The Sun emits three types of ultraviolet radiation, UVA, UVB and UVC, and each has slightly different wavelengths.

The vast majority of the ultraviolet radiation reaching the Earth's surface is UVA, as the atmosphere filters out almost all UVB and UVC radiation. In doing so, the air is heated up and oxygen molecules are split apart into individual atoms. These combine with other oxygen molecules to form ozone, a vital component in the atmosphere.

Over time, ozone has become one of the principal mechanisms that protects the Earth from ultraviolet radiation. In modern times, industrial activity has caused the release of many pollutants, mostly notably CFCs, that have damaged the layer.

A certain amount of exposure is necessary for the human body to be able to produce vitamin D. However, over-exposure to the ultraviolet radiation contained in UVB sunlight can cause skin problems as well as damage to DNA. This can lead to cancer, cataracts forming in the eyes and the immune system being depressed. As a result, many experts promote the use of sunscreen lotions.

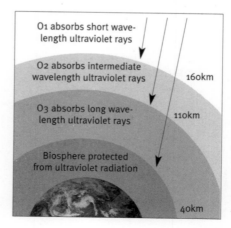

O₁ absorbs short wavelength ultraviolet rays

O₂ absorbs intermediate wavelength ultraviolet rays — 160km

O₃ absorbs long wavelength ultraviolet rays — 110km

Biosphere protected from ultraviolet radiation

40km

Volcanoes

Volcanoes arise as the result of molten rock called magma finding its way to the Earth's surface and pouring out onto the surrounding landscape, often in extremely violent explosions.

Volcanic eruptions occur because magma is under a lot of pressure from the enormous weight of rock above it.

Some of the larger eruptions have discharged so much material into the atmosphere that the world's weather has been changed for many years. This is because the dense clouds of dust and smoke they produce are thick enough to block out the Sun over massive areas.

When Mount Pinatubo in the Philippines blew up in 1991, it is estimated that about 20 million tonnes of sulphur dioxide were released into the upper atmosphere.

An even bigger event occurred in the spring of 1815, when Mount Tambora in Indonesia erupted. It is thought that this was one of the biggest volcanic eruptions of the last 10,000 years, and it blacked out so much of the atmosphere that crops failed across the northern hemisphere, with more than 200,000 people starving to death or being killed by the virulent typhus epidemic that followed.

Volcanic eruptions also occur on other planets. Jupiter's moon is home to several active volcanoes.

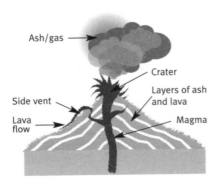

Ash/gas

Crater

Layers of ash and lava

Side vent

Lava flow

Magma

Waste Management

Waste management is the organized collection of domestic or commercial waste and disposing of it in a well-controlled manner.

Best practice waste management – the most environmentally friendly way – involves using sustainable methods. In many countries, however, waste disposal is rudimentary at best.

It also depends on the local geography, as some areas have more space to bury waste than others. Japan, for instance, is a densely populated country with little room to dedicate to landfill operations, and so more waste is burned there than would be the case in larger countries.

From an environmental perspective, the best regimes are those where reuse, recycling, resource recovery and careful disposal are all fully optimized. Landfill sites remain one of the most popular solutions though, and if they are designed and managed well, can have a low impact on the environment.

The leaching of contaminants into the soil is one of the main problems with such methods, but this can, for example, be prevented with membrane liners. Likewise, the release of methane and other atmospheric pollutants can be minimized by capturing them and using them for power generation.

Where waste management is not carried out properly, this can result in all manner of health issues, ranging from the release of toxic substances into the locality to the spread of vermin like rats and cockroaches.

See: *Recycling*, page 157

Weather Front

A weather front marks a line between two masses of air at different pressures.

Weather fronts are important because they often denote significant changes in the weather.

There are several different types of weather fronts. The four basic ones are cold, warm, occluded and stationary.

A cold front is a transition zone in which warm air is being lifted relatively quickly and replaced by cold air. As the warm air rises, it cools and releases any moisture it is carrying as condensation – this forms clouds that are followed by strong precipitation.

A warm front is the reverse of a cold front. Instead, the transition zone has cold air being replaced by warm air – the rate of lifting is much lower and so any precipitation that forms is much milder. An occluded front is where a cold front overtakes a warm one and usually occurs as a result of storm activity.

A stationary front is simply one that has stopped moving.

Weather Map Markings

A cold front (*top left diagram*) is represented by a solid blue line with triangular blocks on the warmer side, indicating its direction of travel.

A warm front (*top right*) is represented by a solid red line with semi-circular blocks on the colder side, indicating its direction of travel.

An occluded front (*bottom left*) is represented by a solid purple line with alternate semi-circular and triangular blocks which point in the direction that the front is moving.

A stationary front (*bottom right*) is represented on a weather map by a solid line with red semi-circular blocks on the colder side, and blue triangular blocks on the warmer side.

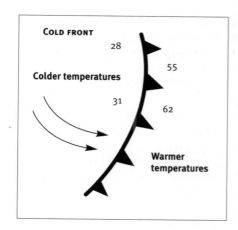

COLD FRONT

28

55

Colder temperatures

31

62

Warmer temperatures

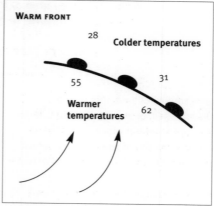

WARM FRONT

28 Colder temperatures

55

31

Warmer temperatures

62

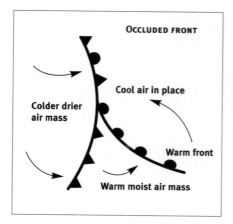

OCCLUDED FRONT

Cool air in place

Colder drier air mass

Warm front

Warm moist air mass

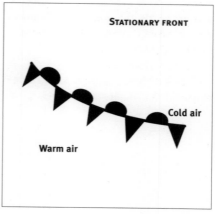

STATIONARY FRONT

Cold air

Warm air

Wetland

A wetland is an area of land that is not sufficiently covered with water to be considered an aquatic environment, but is so waterlogged that it cannot be labelled truly terrestrial.

Examples of wetlands include marshes, peat bogs, swamps, mires and other similar places, with these often being found as boundary zones between dry land and stretches of water.

For a location to be categorized as a true wetland, it must be able to support a population of hydrophyte vegetation. In other words, temporarily flooded land does not count – it must be inundated for enough of the year for wetland plants to survive there.

Many such areas support a wide range of animals and plants and so are extremely valuable environmental resources. They can also act as buffer zones when severe precipitation occurs and, in doing so, prevent factories, homes and other important buildings from being flooded.

Unfortunately, in recent years many have been drained for use by agriculture, industry or for residential and leisure purposes. As a result of this, sustained efforts are being made in many countries by conservation bodies to restore some of the lost wetland areas and to preserve the remaining ones.

See: *Flooding*, page 81; *Peat Bog*, page 145; *Precipitation*, pages 152–153

Whaling

Whaling is the process of finding and killing cetaceans – whales, dolphins and porpoises – for commercial purposes or as a food source.

The hunting of cetaceans is an activity that goes back many thousands of years to prehistoric times.

At this early stage, however, the methods of hunting were somewhat rudimentary. One popular means of killing was to trap the whales in a small bay and then force them into a small area where they were then shot with arrows.

In the open sea, early whaling was significantly constrained by the limitations of the rudimentary boats that were available to the hunters. Consequently, very few were killed relative to the world population of whales.

In more recent times, however, this situation has changed dramatically.

At the start of the Industrial Revolution, both the weaponry and the navigational equipment began to change almost beyond recognition. Demand for whale products such as oil and meat rose with the increasing human population.

Over the 19th and 20th centuries the rapid rate of killing meant that the numbers of many species of whales crashed. In response to a public outcry against whaling, the International Whaling Commission was established in 1946 in order to try and regulate the industry. Certain areas were designated as whale sanctuaries, and many endangered species were protected.

Currently, there is a moratorium on whaling in place, but some countries, such as Norway, continue to kill Minke whales commercially.

See: *Cetaceans*, page 44; *Extinction*, page 79; *Fishing*, page 80

Wildfire

Wildfires have been a natural part of many ecosystems for tens of millions of years as the result of such phenomena as lightning strikes.

Many regions suffer from wildfires, including the United States, Canada, the Australian bush and the South African veldt. One of the biggest fires occurred in 1871 near Peshtigo, Wisconsin, when more than 2,500,000 acres (810,000 hectares) were destroyed and 1,500 lives lost.

Plants and animals have evolved over the millennia to cope with the occurrence of wildfires. These include such examples as the species of tree that needs to be exposed to the heat of a fire before its seed pods can ripen.

Although many wildfires are started through natural causes, particularly lightning, in practice human activity is responsible for most of the wildfires that are seen today. Some are deliberate acts of vandalism; others are accidental.

In periods of prolonged drought the underbrush can become so dry that the slightest spark can start a fire. If the wind is in a direction that favours the flames, an enormous conflagration can occur quickly. Consequently, strict precautions have to be taken by anyone passing through affected areas

In British Columbia, Canada, and Arizona in the United States, the authorities have undertaken extensive fire protection programmes. As well as ensuring that the various fire protection agencies are working efficiently with each other, these programmes aim to raise public awareness about the causes and prevention of wildfires through the use of such things as newspaper advertisements, leaflets, posters and presentations in schools.

Wind

Wind is a natural part of the world's weather system. It arises as the result of large masses of air with differing atmospheric pressures flowing towards or away from one another.

Humankind has exploited wind for thousands of years. In the earliest times it was used to drive vessels, and after that the next main development was the invention of the windmill for grinding corn or driving machinery. These days it is used to generate electricity.

Differences in atmospheric pressure are typically caused by the way in which the Sun heats some areas more than it does others. For example, seas and oceans take longer to warm up than the land does. Likewise, cloud cover can make a big difference to the speed with which the air is heated, and the same is true of mountains and snow fields. Since hot air is light and cold air is dense, when the two meet, the warmer mass rises over the colder one, and this movement generates the phenomenon we refer to as wind. Meteorologists usually categorize air that flows horizontally as wind, whereas they label air that moves vertically as a current.

There are four major categories of winds: the prevailing winds, the seasonal winds, the local winds, and the cyclonic and anticyclonic winds, which include cyclones, hurricanes and tornadoes.

Winds are categorized by strength on the Beaufort Scale, and go from 0, which indicates dead calm, up to 12, which is classed as a hurricane.

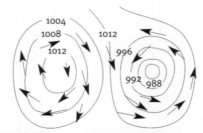

Wind is caused by air flowing from high pressure to low pressure. Its direction is influenced by the Earth's rotation.

Wind Power

*Wind power is a form of sustainable energy that
has both advocates and detractors.*

Wind power has been used for many centuries since the time when the Babylonians and Chinese, among others, used it to power sailing craft and pump water for irrigation purposes. In the Middle Ages wind power was also used to grind seeds into flour.

Until the dawn of the Industrial Revolution in the mid 18th century, the methods of exploiting wind power had changed little and when steam power came along it was more or less superseded overnight. As a result, it disappeared as a terrestrial power source in most developed countries until the 20th century, when the depleted fossil fuel stocks made an alternative, more environmentally friendly source of power important.

Wind power is mostly produced on wind farms, which became increasingly more popular from the 1990s onwards. Initially very expensive to produce, wind power has became more affordable as technical innovations have increased its efficiency. Wind power also does not produce any atmospheric pollutants nor does it waste resources. Today, electricity generated by wind turbines is comparable in cost to that produced by more conventional methods.

However, critics argue that wind is not a predictable resource, and that for the majority of the time most sites do not reach viable working speeds. They also claim that manufacturing wind turbines is environmentally unfriendly and that wind farms are ugly.

Many governments globally support the use of wind power, however. According to the British Wind Energy Association (BWEA) primary legislation exists to ensure that 10 per cent of Britain's renewable energy will come from wind power by 2010 and 15 per cent by 2015.

World Heritage Site

In 2008, there were 851 World Heritage Sites forming part of the cultural and natural heritage considered to be of outstanding universal value.

In 1972, the United Nations Educational, Scientific and Cultural Organization (UNESCO) adopted an international treaty called the Convention Concerning the Protection of the World Cultural and Natural Heritage. More than 180 countries have ratified the convention. The World Heritage programme was established as a result of it by which designated cultural and natural sites around the world, nominated by an international committee, are protected and preserved for prosterity.

Until the end of 2004, sites were selected on the basis of six cultural and four natural criteria. Following the adoption of the revised Operational Guidelines for the Implementation of the World Heritage Convention, sites must meet 1 of 10 criteria, which include representing a '*masterpiece of creative human genius*' and containing '*the most important and significant natural habitats for in-situ conservation of biological diversity*'.

The places listed as World Heritage Sites include various archaeological, geophysical and ethnological locations that are categorized as either natural heritage or cultural sites in countries.

The cost of protecting the listed places is met by the member states, but only developing countries are able to apply for monetary assistance.

Examples of World Heritage Sites include Stonehenge and Hadrian's Wall in the United Kingdom; the Great Barrier Reef and the Sydney Opera House in Australia; and the Everglades, the Yosemite National Park and the Statue of Liberty in the United States.

Zooplankton

Zooplankton encompasses the various forms of animals that spend some or all of their lives either floating or drifting in water.

Typically, zooplankton organisms have very limited control over their movement through water, relying on local or oceanic currents for transportation from place to place.

Zooplankton range in size from microscopic creatures such as protozoans, foraminifera, radiolarians and rotifers, to large animals like jellyfish, which can be many metres in length. The bigger forms are sometimes referred to as 'macro-zooplankton'. Many of the smaller forms are actually the larvae of well known animals such as molluscs, crabs, shrimp, lobsters, fish and so on.

The collective scientific term for this class of organisms is 'meroplankton'. The various creatures that comprise the zooplankton play a vital role in the environment, being major consumers of phytoplankton as well as being the primary sources of food for many other animals, from corals to the Whale Shark – the biggest fish in the world.

The density of zooplankton can be used as an important indicator of a particular ecosystem's health. If this is higher than normal, it is typically a sign of too many nutrients in the water. Conversely, if it is too low, it may indicate fouling from toxic pollution or some other specific problem.

See: *Environment*, page 77; *Fishing*, page 80; *Molluscs*, page 129

What You Can Do For the Environment

The state of the environment is the responsibility of every person on the planet. We can all do our little bit to protect the wellbeing of the world we live in.

Although there is still a significant debate raging about whether global warming and climate change are caused by humankind or by nature, there is no doubt at all that the huge increase in the human population over recent years has taken a terrible toll on the environment. As individuals, it is frustrating to feel that there is little one can do to influence the political stance of the world's various governments. There is, however, quite a lot that can be done that *will* have a direct and beneficial effect on local ecosystems.

The sections below examine simple measures which, if adopted by enough people, would at least help to offset some of the damage caused by our everyday lives.

There are a wealth of tips and general advice available in today's media, but it is important to remember that every one of the suggestions made must be both practical to implement and cost-effective to run if they are going to provide long-lasting benefits. If they fail to meet these two crucial criteria, they will fail to deliver any significant impact and will be a waste of time, money and effort.

THE GARDEN

One of the best ways to reduce your household's impact on the environment is to create your own mini ecosystem in your garden. By encouraging wild animals and plants to thrive there, you are providing an important refuge for a wide range of different organisms.

Vegetables

An excellent way to become more environmentally friendly is to grow some of your own vegetables. This means both a regular supply of fresh organic produce for little cost and fewer journeys to the shops. This results in lower fuel consumption by food suppliers transporting fewer products to large supermarkets.

Pest control

If you choose to plant up your own vegetable patch, you will soon discover that you are not the only one who likes to eat your produce. It will seem that every pest for miles around has made it a personal mission to gnaw their way through your prized plants before you are able to harvest them. Plenty of old-school gardeners will tell you that the best solution to slugs and snails is to use pest control pellets. Although some of these pellets are now far less toxic than they used to be, the best way to deal with slugs and snails is simply to go out after dark and remove the offending beasts by hand with the aid of a torch. That way there is no risk of birds or other animals being contaminated by consuming the bodies of slugs and snails that have died after eating poisonous pellets. Removing any nearby weeds, as well as any objects that these pests can hide under such as stones or plant pots, will also help to reduce their numbers.

An excellent way of reducing the problems of pests is to keep a few bantams. These are small chickens that can be let loose in your garden during the day, where they will search out and eat vast numbers of undesirable creatures. It is important to ensure that you have good fences so that they cannot stray into danger; at night, simply return them to their hutch where they can be locked up out of the way of predators such as foxes and rats. One bonus is that you will not only reduce any need for pesticides, but you will also get a regular supply of free-range eggs, albeit small ones!

Water

All gardens need to have a sufficient supply of water, but in some areas this may be in short supply, especially at the height of summer when your plants will need it the most. It is therefore important to ensure that you do not waste the water you have. Some of the measures that you can take are very simple; instead of using a hose, for instance, you can use a watering can which uses much less water. Watering efficiently, either first thing in the morning or last thing at night, will maximize the impact on your plants and ensure that the moisture has a chance to drain away into the soil and reach the roots before it is evaporated away by the Sun. A thick layer of mulch, such as your own, home-produced garden compost, placed around the base of your plants will also prevent the soil from drying out.

If you have the room to do so, it is a good idea to install some devices to collect rainwater, for example, the most common method is to fit a water butt on the end of one of the drainpipes from your roof. If you choose to do this, it is worthwhile covering it with a wire mesh that will still allow the birds to drink from it, but will prevent other animals from falling in and drowning. Before purchasing any such storage systems, it is worth checking with your local authority to see if they are running any subsidized schemes; they often sell water butts at lower prices to encourage their use. The water that you collect in these vessels will not only reduce the demand on the local supply, but will also be better for your plants. This is because it will be free from the chemicals, such as chlorine, that are used to keep tap water free of dangerous pathogens. If your supply is metered, it will also save you money.

Another way to reduce demand on your local utility is by using greywater to irrigate your garden. This is simply the term given to any water that is discharged from sinks, baths, washing machines and basins; it does not, however, include that from toilets. Greywater can generally be collected relatively easily by making a few simple modifications to your outflow pipes. It is important to check, however, that any waste water used on edible plants comes from suitable sources. If in any doubt, refer to an expert before you, or anyone else, becomes ill from eating contaminated food.

Birds

To make the most of any avian visitors to your garden, especially those who might choose to build their nests there, it is vital to ensure that predators cannot catch and kill them. In the United Kingdom, the worst culprits by a long way are domestic cats, Grey Squirrels and magpies. Every cat should be fitted with a collar and bell; whilst this does not remove the risk of them killing valuable wildlife, it does, however, lower the chances. Many owners will insist that their beloved pet would never kill anything, but it is a sad fact that cats are predators that have evolved to hunt small creatures, and most will do so if given the chance. Although it is nature's way, cats are animals of the jungle, forest and savannah, not the suburban garden. It is therefore very important to ensure that birds are only fed in places where the risk of attack has been minimized.

Grey Squirrels, magpies and many other corvids, such as crows, will readily raid birds' nests and eat any eggs or baby chicks they can find. It is thus a good idea to fit properly built nest boxes. Check the entrance size of the holes though as most bird species will only use nest boxes if they are a certain diameter. To find out what size is best for your area, you should consult the advice given by local conservation bodies. If there are lots of woodpeckers in the vicinity, there will be a significant risk of your nest boxes being broken into and chicks inside being eaten. This can be prevented by fitting metal rings around the entrance holes. Bats can also benefit from boxes being fitted in suitable places and, once again, local specialists can advise on how and where any boxes should be sited.

Wildlife
The amount of scope you have for assisting your local wildlife will depend to a large extent on the size and location of your garden. If you have sufficient room, keeping one area uncultivated will help establish a refuge for many different species of plants and animals. You will still have to manage this area, however, to ensure that it is not overgrown by unwanted vegetation such as Japanese Knotweed.

Ponds can be especially beneficial, although it is not a good idea to keep fish in them as they will consume many of the organisms that are necessary for the survival of species such as frogs, toads, newts, dragonflies, water beetles and so on. In cold periods it is important to make sure that if ice forms the birds are still able to access fresh water as without sufficient moisture intake they will die very quickly.

Insects
Although some insects are significant garden pests, many others are extremely beneficial; without pollinators, for instance, most flowering plants would be unable to set seed. Examples of such creatures include butterflies, moths, bees and hover flies. The best way to attract them into your garden is to cultivate suitable plants. One of the best

known is buddleia, but others include valerian, ice-plants, lavender and tobacco plants. Ivy is an excellent plant to have in the garden, especially when it has matured to the point where it produces flowers as these are a rich source of nutrients for many insects. During the winter, however, its evergreen leaves provide an excellent place for many vulnerable creatures to hibernate.

Other insects are voracious predators on the major pests; ladybirds and lacewings, for instance, consume vast numbers of greenfly. The best way to encourage them is to provide suitable hibernating places; stacks of old logs work well, as do the specially-made structures that are sold in garden centres. It is not just insects that seek out garden pests, however, as frogs, toads, lizards and hedgehogs will all eat slugs as well as many other unwanted creatures. Likewise, several species of birds are the gardener's friend; thrushes, for instance, are masters at finding and eating snails. The evidence for this can often be seen in the form of piles of broken snail shells.

Pesticides

When planning an environmentally friendly garden, one of the most basic tenets is to avoid the use of chemicals such as pesticides, herbicides and fertilizers, except those which have been proven to have few or no harmful impacts. Glyphosate weedkillers, for example, can be used as a last resort when manual removal has failed to achieve the desired effect. Whenever any such substances are used, it is vital that instructions are read and followed carefully. While some pesticides are available that are derived from plant sources, many pests can be controlled by using natural means. In recent years, for example, nematode worms have become a popular alternative to chemical treatments. These are parasites which burrow into the flesh of the pests, killing them from the inside. They are readily available from many garden suppliers, and are simply sprinkled over the affected plants and left to their own devices.

Solar power

Before buying any electric lights or water features, check to see if solar-powered alternatives are available. If they are, then it is worth installing them as they will consume fewer resources. It is important to think carefully before replacing any existing devices, however, as the cost to the environment is much greater than keeping the ones you already have. This philosophy can be extended throughout the rest of your lifestyle, too.

IN THE HOUSE

Almost everyone in the developed world could make significant improvements to the ways in which their households are run if they wanted to. The biggest saving from an environmental perspective is probably to stop buying unnecessary consumer goods. These days most of the products concerned are made in countries that pay scant regard to the environment, and anything that fuels the trade is potentially harmful both to the supplies of natural resources and to the global ecosystem.

Efficiency

In most kitchens, there are several appliances that consume resources such as energy and water. The efficiency of many of these can often be improved by ensuring that they are regularly serviced, and that they are run on the most appropriate settings. This not only cuts down on unnecessary usage, but can save money as well. Although new models usually have their efficiency ratings prominently displayed, it is far better to keep your existing equipment – if it is running well – than to keep replacing it. Most appliances are there for convenience purposes only; tumble dryers, for instance, are found in most modern houses. They are, however, very wasteful from an energy perspective; it may take longer to dry your clothes on a line or a rack, but it does not use any electricity to do so. If you do have to replace any appliances, check to see what the local opportunities for recycling are. Reuse is far better for the environment than disposal.

Energy-saving activities

There are many other ways to save energy around the house; setting the washing machine to run at a lower temperature is an excellent example. Turning off devices that normally sit on standby mode is another, as is making sure that all dishwashers and washing machines are only used when they have a full load. Fridges and freezers should not only be adjusted correctly, but they should also be defrosted regularly to ensure that they are working in their most efficient state.

One of the main forms of energy wastage is through poorly insulated houses. A large amount of heat is lost due to a lack of adequate insulation. The amount of draughts that blow around doors can often be reduced by using sealing strips. Double glazing can make a huge difference to the warmth of a house, especially if special low heat-loss glass is used. For those who have the money to invest in alternative sources of energy, there are many choices in the marketplace. These include wind turbines, solar panels, ground source heat pumps and so on. Before buying any of these, however, it is vital that sufficient research is carried out. The sales brochures always make claims that sound wonderful but often these turn out to be so cleverly worded that they are meaningless when examined carefully. Some home wind turbine kits, for instance, offer the chance of generating free electricity. When the facts are checked though, it is clear that the purchase cost can never be recovered as the equipment is not designed to last for the required duration.

Although reducing energy usage is of primary importance, there are also many other ways in which the domestic household can be run in a more environmentally friendly manner. A good example of this would be the choice of paints and varnishes. Many contain volatile organic compounds which can be present in the air of your house for several years after application. Certain components within these chemicals are toxic and so are best avoided. Emulsion paints are generally fine to use, but most oil-based gloss paints and many varnishes are not. There are a lot of eco-friendly alternatives available nowadays, so there is little excuse to use potentially harmful materials. If in doubt, read the label carefully, and if it does not tell you what you want to know, either ask someone with the relevant expertize or use the internet to find out. Getting rid of empty or part-used tins of paint is another matter that needs to be carefully thought about, as careless disposal can release noxious substances into the environment. Most recycling centres have dedicated disposal facilities for such materials, so it is worth taking the trouble to use them.

CARS

One of the main mantras of those in the eco-active brigade is that everyone should use public transport or bicycles rather than drive cars. These people do the subject of environmentalism no favours at all, as the vast majority of the world's inhabitants do not live close to their workplaces, or in areas that are well-serviced by buses or trains. It is all very well for city-dwellers to lecture everyone else about their ability to do without their own internal combustion engines, but this immediately antagonizes those who cannot. As a result, they are far less likely to take on board the really important aspects of reducing their impact on the environment.

Although many people would have us all believe that where cars are concerned, the main source of harm to the environment comes from their exhaust emissions, this is, in reality, a long way wide of the mark. By far the biggest environmental consequences are due to a vehicle's initial manufacture and then its final disposal. It is far more environmentally friendly to keep a car on the road for a long period than it is to keep changing it every few years for a newer model. Some would argue that modern cars

are more efficient, and therefore generate fewer pollutants. While this may be the case in some instances, many older cars respond well to the fitment of modern parts, and so can be easily improved at modest cost.

These vehicles also tend to have little in the way of electronic systems, and so only require replacement when major body repair is no longer economic. When this stage is reached, it is often possible to dismantle the vehicle and re-use the majority of its components as spares to help keep other similar models on the road. Before too long, car manufacturers are going to have to re-think their policies if they are to continue selling vehicles. The current ethos of disposable models is scandalous from an environmental perspective, and a return to longer-lasting designs would be a major step in the right direction.

Many diesel vehicles can be run on vegetable oil with little or no modification; some even perform more efficiently, producing fewer pollutants, and running more reliably. Others can be made to run on biodiesel for little capital outlay. Both methods help to reduce our dependency on fossil fuels.

Acknowledgements

I should like to thank all those at Focus Publishing for giving me the opportunity to write this book. I am particularly indebted to Vicky Hales-Dutton for her patient editing of the text and Heather McMillan for her excellent illustrations.

I dedicate this book to my daughters, Carina and Gemma, as well as to my fiancée Claire and her children, Hugo and Sophia.

Patrick Hook
Witheridge, Devon
January 2008

PICTURE AND CHART CREDITS
The chart on page 159 (*Renewable Energy*) comes from *The Renewable Energy Annual* (2005 edition), courtesy of the Energy Information Administration.

Index

Index

Index

Index